MILLIONAIRE REAL ESTATE
SUCCESS STRATEGIES

MILLIONAIRE REAL ESTATE SUCCESS STRATEGIES

What They Forgot to Teach You in School

Johnny E. Lynum II

NEW DEGREE PRESS

COPYRIGHT © 2021 JOHNNY E. LYNUM II

MILLIONAIRE REAL ESTATE SUCCESS STRATEGIES

What They Forgot to Teach You in School

ISBN

978-1-63730-991-9   *Paperback*

978-1-63730-788-5   *Kindle Ebook*

979-8-88504-018-1   *Digital Ebook*

*For my dad Johnnie and my mom Ruth, who
made me into the man I am today.*

CONTENTS

———

INTRODUCTION

———

"Success is the freedom to live your life as the great big fat adventure it is—and the wisdom to understand that all you have to do is to choose to do so."

JOHN JANTSCH, AUTHOR OF *THE REFERRAL ENGINE*

I pray this book finds you in a place of abundance in your life and your real estate journey! If it doesn't, that's okay too. I have been there in my life, as well as almost every successful real estate investor's story mentioned in this book. It's not about where you start in life, but where you will accomplish the goals you have set for yourself!

This book will assist you in taking your real estate investing business to the next level, purchasing your first investment property, or even buying your first home to live in. You will see first hand the different strategies successful investors use to invest in single-family and multifamily deals. You will learn great marketing strategies to find off-market deals for 40 percent to 50 percent of their after-repair value. Before we get into the hands-on tactics, you will learn how the millionaire habits of goal setting, taking action, networking, and having grit will create sustained success in all areas of your life! Are you ready for the journey?

I wrote this book to help as many people as possible become wealthy. Why? Because you and your family deserve it. There is an abundance of wealth in this world, yet so many have limiting beliefs about finding wealth and happiness in life. With faith and a little hard work, you too can secure wealth for generations to come and secure your American Dream. The "American Dream" phrase first appeared in the 1931 bestseller, *Epic of America*. The author viewed the American Dream as "that dream of a land in which life should be better and richer and fuller for everyone, with opportunity for each according to ability or achievement." This was a noble dream, but it hasn't played out that way for most.

Since America's inception, immigrants have flocked to its shores to experience the unrivaled freedom to aspire for greatness and the opportunity to achieve the "American Dream." Today, the United States stands as the most powerful country in the world with the world's largest economy producing an annual gross domestic product of over twenty-two trillion dollars. Furthermore, it houses the largest portion of the world's billionaires and the largest share of Fortune Global 500 companies. Despite these exceptional levels of wealth and power, many Americans are yet to experience the American Dream.

So, just how bad is it? The Pew Research Center performed a study back in 2016 and identified a few disturbing trends. The wealth gap between America's richest and poorest families more than doubled from 1989 to 2016. These metrics clearly highlight that the average American lacks the knowledge to build wealth. Is this an anomaly? Furthermore, they found the top 5 percent of the wealthiest families held 248 times as much wealth as the median. When they looked at the poorest 20 percent of families, they found their median wealth was either zero or negative in most of the years examined. Knowing this, you won't be surprised to hear that when it comes to "retirement," nearly half of all American families have no retirement savings at all.

How did this happen? How did the greatest nation in the world leave so many people behind? We will briefly examine the different causes that led us to this puzzle and deep dive into those foundational changes you can make in your life and the real estate vehicles you can leverage to build generational wealth. Furthermore, I will share the stories of everyday Americans who have used these same strategies to build wealth. Knowing how to build wealth is critical regardless of where you are in life. Fortunately, the principles laid out in this book can make you a successful real estate investor if you decide to take action. A 2017 survey from Fidelity Investments found that 88 percent of millionaires are self-made, and only 12 percent inherited significant money. If you don't have a rich uncle, you need to take action! Do you know what that action is? It's real estate! Here's another fact for you, 77 percent of millionaire investors say they own real estate! This is not just correlation; there is causation in this fact, too.

So far, I have explained primarily about the financial rewards from real estate investing, but is there more? I have found success to be personal, and it can only be defined by the individual. However, we often focus on a well-paying job, money, and material items to define success for our lives, only to be disappointed when we become enlightened on our true purpose later in life. Some call it your passion or your "why" in life, but it's all centered around finding your purpose.

Take a second and consider those who society deems successful by only considering their bank account and expensive possessions. If success were solely based on money, then CEOs, athletes, and celebrities would be exempt from experiencing personal struggles or lows in life. Life coach and best-selling author Tony Robbins said, "I've found success is 80 percent psychology and 20 percent skills. The psychological aspect is dependent on how much you grow, improve, and push yourself beyond what you thought was possible." Being able to get over my personal fears and limiting beliefs catapulted my real estate business. Unfortunately, the strategies I'm going to lay out in this book aren't handed out in a textbook or during some structured college course. If anyone knows this first hand, it's me.

I grew up in LA...not Los Angeles—Lower Alabama, outside the three-traffic-light town of Grove Hill. My father was a Baptist pastor and a small appliance and TV repair business owner. My mom was a phlebotomist at the local town hospital. My parents worked hard to make sure my sister and I had everything we needed in life. In my hometown, success was somewhat limited to landing a good job at one of the local paper mills, which is not a bad profession. However, my parents ingrained in me success was leaving our small town, going to college, and choosing a corporate office job. Today, my definition of success has shifted to generating enough passive income to pay all my monthly expenses while having the time freedom to do whatever I want. Real estate was my vehicle that got me there.

After finishing high school with multiple scholarship offers, I attended The University of Alabama, graduated with an electrical engineering degree with minors in math and physics, and was commissioned as a lieutenant in the US Air Force. Out of the gate, I was laser-focused on my career. I wanted to be the best officer and engineer the Air Force had ever seen. I aimed to be the first person in the office and the last one out the door. After sitting out one year of school, I started graduate school to complete my master's in business administration.

I thought working hard would get me promoted and ultimately provide job security. I was book smart and knew how to be a great employee, but I knew very little about money, investing, or real estate—all critical pillars to building generational wealth. As I grew in rank, pay, and responsibility, I still didn't feel truly fulfilled in my life, and at times, I felt borderline depressed about it because I knew I had so much potential. The entrepreneurial thrill of building a successful business was tugging at my heart hard.

I recalled how as a teenager my dad told me that if you wanted to be rich, you couldn't do it working for someone else your entire life. This point was really driven home for me when I negotiated an over-two-hundred-million-dollar contract for the Air Force that saved the government over ten million dollars, but there's no such thing as an end of the year bonus for military officers. This experience motivated me to bet on myself and start my own business to buy, renovate, and sell houses. With help from my wonderful wife, Melissa, we decided to take action. We found our first deal a few weeks later and haven't stopped since!

Flipping houses and building a multi-million-dollar rental portfolio didn't happen overnight. An old saying goes, "When the student is ready, the teacher will appear." By choosing to read this book, clearly you are ready to take action, too. I have no doubt you have what it takes to use the principles I will teach you to become a successful real estate investor.

I will share my personal experiences and those of other successful investors who have broken free from the chains of working hard to make someone else rich and ultimately redefined success for their lives. For me, success is having the freedom to live life on my terms without trading time for money as well as inspiring others to achieve their goals. Kobe Bryant said, "The most important thing is to try and inspire people so that they can be great in whatever they want to do." If you're serious about real estate investing, finding your "why" is critical to long-term commitment.

You will learn the same habits and strategies utilized by the wealthy, so you can leverage them to invest in real estate and build generational wealth successfully. I know it may be hard to believe that you, too, can become a millionaire investor because I was in your shoes before. Real estate investing isn't rocket science. I can personally attest to the viability and effectiveness of the principles and strategies laid out on the pages of this book. I leveraged these same principles and frameworks en route to achieving a seven-figure net worth, a multi-million-dollar real estate portfolio, and multiple real estate-focused companies—all in a few short years while still serving full-time, active duty in the US Air Force.

At the end of each one of the chapters, I included an implementation section. This section is included to allow you an opportunity to reflect on the themes from the chapter and determine how you can implement them into your life. The stories and concepts included throughout the book are great exemplars to highlight the success of others, but my goal is to make it personal for you. Once you complete reading this book, you will have your own personal roadmap to success.

I can't guarantee the journey will be easy, but I guarantee all the hard work will be worthwhile. You will learn to set and conquer goals that will help you *live* this life, not just wander through it. Les Brown, a famous motivational speaker and author, said, "The graveyard is the richest place on earth because it is here that you will find all the hopes and dreams that were never fulfilled, the books that were never written, the songs that were never sung, the inventions that were never shared, the cures that were never discovered, all because someone was too afraid to take that first step, keep with the problem, or determined to carry out their dream." Success leaves a trail. Let's follow that trail and create your own personal roadmap to achieving *your* American Dream! Let's begin the journey.

CHAPTER 1

CURRENT STATE OF AFFAIRS

———

"Identify your problems, but give your power and energy to solutions."

TONY ROBBINS

AMERICA TODAY

At no point ever in American history has there been a better time to be alive. People are living longer with better access to health care along with the proliferation of technology. Technology has fundamentally changed nearly every facet of our lives—from purchasing groceries to surgeons performing remote surgeries from over five thousand miles away. Yet many Americans lack the basic foundational skills and strategies necessary to thrive and lead a successful life. I'm not necessarily talking only about finances, but just the ability to live comfortably while providing the opportunity for greater achievement for the next generation. Unfortunately, most of the schools in America's education system don't teach the principles of financial literacy and the strategies to build generational wealth. Depending on your economic environment, there is no guarantee you will receive the critical information at home either.

Today's entrepreneurs have certainly benefited and blossomed in this new era. One great example is Mikaila Ulmer, the eleven-year-old Austin, Texas, native who created Bee Sweet Lemonade, an eleven-million-dollar lemonade business. She started at four years old using her great-grandmother Helen's lemonade recipe. In 2015 at the age of ten, Whole Foods Market received information concerning her effort and started selling her product in thirty-two stores and four states. Later that year, she appeared on Shark Tank. She secured a $60,000 investment from Damon Johns, FUBU CEO and investor. Two years later, a consortium of former and current American football players invested $800,000! If a preteen can raise over $800,000 for a lemonade business, then adult should be a savvy entrepreneur and investor.

Numerous studies and surveys have been performed about financial literacy and the lack of savings in the United States. During my research, one great study that I found was by Daniel Zapp at EVERFI, whose mission is to provide the missing layer of education by leveraging technology. From 2012 to 2018, EVERFI, sponsored by AIG, surveyed over thirty thousand college students from over four hundred and forty institutions across forty-four states. Their results were scathing! Overall, the results suggested the college students surveyed suffered from a lack of financial capability long before accepting their first job post-college. Furthermore, they cited the necessity for employers to be aware of the group's attitudes and behaviors regarding money since it could potentially impact job performance.

Let's take a quick look at some of the stats. Fifty-three percent said they were least prepared to manage their money compared to managing time, finding resources, keeping up with coursework, and staying organized. Only 35 percent of the sample of adults reported ever having taken a personal finance course in high school. To determine each student's level of financial capability, they asked six basic financial knowledge questions centered around credit history, net worth, interest rates, and student loans. The respondents struggled to answer the basic questions correctly, with the average respondent only answering two of the six multiple-choice questions correctly. Looking even more broadly, Lusuadi and colleagues found that only 48 percent of all American adults could identify at least half of the correct answers to a set of financial literacy questions.

MY STORY

I can personally attest to the lack of financial literacy taught in most schools and American households. My parents were hard-working folks who wanted the best for their kids, which is no different than any other parent. After growing up in rural Texas and Alabama, my mother and father moved to Detroit, Michigan, in the late 1960s. So, when my dad decided to leave Detroit in 1989, it was a tough adjustment for everyone.

Although they weren't college graduates, my parents instilled in me success was going to college, obtaining a degree, and getting a good job working for a good company. Thirty years or so ago, this was the case, but today's economy has changed. As Les Brown has stated in multiple interviews, today's economy has gone from brick and mortar to click and order!

Despite living in a quiet small town, my parents both knew from experience there was a lot more to life than what I was exposed to every day. They always motivated and encouraged my sister and me to do our best in school as that was our ticket to get out of our small town. They taught me about integrity, hard work, and to live by my word. They didn't know about the stock market, personal financial statements, self-directed retirement accounts and real estate investing, but they gave me the intangibles I needed to be successful.

Lucky enough for me, I was always wired differently and wanted to win at whatever I started. I hated losing almost as badly as Kobe Bryant did. I can still remember who I lost the fourth-grade spelling bee to and how I cried like a baby. After seeing the struggles of my parents and the long days they put in to provide for the family, failure was not an option. We didn't have a lot, but I thank the Lord we never missed a meal!

I finished third in my graduating class with a 4.2 GPA and as the most valuable player of the varsity basketball team with multiple academic scholarships, including a four-year Army Reserve Officer Training Corps (ROTC) scholarship. A month before graduation, I declined the Army scholarship for an opportunity to compete for a four-year Air Force ROTC scholarship once I arrived on campus at the University of Alabama. In the grand scheme of things, I had a successful résumé going into college, but looking back on it, I was still missing some of those key strategies necessary for long-term success. Good grades and smartness don't guarantee success in life any more than having a hammer makes you a carpenter.

Fast forward to my college graduation. I had seventeen years of education, an electrical engineering degree, and a government job, yet I had a failing financial IQ. When I graduated in August 2005, I had a sub-600 credit score and needed a family relative to cosign my first apartment. I had no clue how credit worked and how my lack of creditworthiness could negatively impact my ability to get my life started on my own.

It was a humbling and embarrassing feeling, but one that was necessary for me to make a conscious effort to do better and start to figure out everything I hadn't been taught that I desperately needed to be successful. I began to research credit repair companies and other online information on how to fix my credit. This was one of the best decisions I ever made since I was able to increase my credit score to 680 in less than one year and purchase my first home.

To be successful as a real estate investor, you must have the right mindset regarding money. Money drives everything we do in our society regardless of our religion, race, ethnicity, or where we live. Growing up as a Southern Baptist, I always remember hearing the scripture, 1 Timothy 6:10: "The love of money is the root of all evil. It's not the money that's evil, but the heart of the person with it who falls in love with it." There is plenty more misinformation out there when it comes to money. You have heard them all! A penny saved is a...save for a...another day, another...money doesn't grow...See, you have heard them all!

Wealthy people don't work for money; they make their money work for them. Therefore, the concept of investing is so important to pick up early in life because it allows you to escape the trap of working every day for a single source of income at a job that could fire you at any moment. Many people say real estate investing is risky, but I argue that working for a single employer to take care of your family is risky.

Today, millions of Americans live paycheck to paycheck and are forced to take on bad debt through credit cards and high-interest loans. According to Nielsen data, the American Payroll Association, CareerBuilder, and the National Endowment for Financial Education, somewhere between 50 percent and 78 percent of employees earn just enough money to pay their bills each month. From a 2017 Federal Reserve economic report, 40 percent of Americans don't have enough money on hand to cover a $400 emergency expense. It highlighted that when confronted with such an expense, those Americans would be forced to sell something or go into debt.

This highlights the dire need for more financial literacy to better assist citizens with managing their finances and becoming astute investors. Conversely, an enormous amount of financial information and knowledge is available through the internet, books, podcasts, and websites to teach concepts and strategies. So, why do so many people still miss the mark when it comes to financial literacy? It could be a lack of hope or motivation; for many, it comes down to having assistance with getting started and the actual implementation of the information.

Society has sold us so many stereotypes that lock us into dead-end jobs chasing a paycheck to only barely meet our basic needs. They tell us we should work, live below our means until sixty-five, and retire and enjoy ourselves. Wall Street and the financial institutions tell us the only retirement option we have is investing in the stock market with our IRA/401Ks. Not one of us knows how long we have here on earth, so why in the hell would I wait until I'm sixty-five to start spending my money and living. It's hard to break away from conventional wisdom and choose the path less traveled to obtain true freedom and success. Luckily, there is hope!

CORPORATE AMERICA TO MULTIFAMILY INVESTOR

In spring 2021, I met John Casmon, a phenomenal guy who had a successful marketing career but knew there had to be more to life than trading his time for money and being totally dependent on an employer for all his income. We sat down on a video call to chat and talk about his story and how he transitioned out of corporate America to become a full-time real estate investor.

John shared with me his original thought process when it came to success. "When it all started out, I was told the path to success was to go to college, graduate, get a good job and work that job until you retire, and then you can go off and live a wild adventure. I was the first one in my family to go to college and graduate, so I spent a lot of my formative years trying to figure out what success looked like because I didn't have anyone breathing down my neck telling me I had to do it a certain way. I read *Rich Dad Poor Dad* like a lot of people, and that really opened my eyes to the way money works and about both business and investment income. One of the things in the book that stood out to me was, you should work a job to develop a skill, and once you develop that skill, you should move on."

John was extremely hungry and wanted to ensure his hunger came through when interviewing and building relationships with different companies. You can't teach people passion, grit, or dedication. He graduated and worked in the family business for a while before being recruited by General Motors. "I was doing stuff working with the Pontiac brand and working with musicians like 50 Cent and Pussycat Dolls and other clients like Maxim, NCAA video games, working with Kirk Herbstreit and Chris Fowler as a twenty-six-year-old marketing executive. I was on top of the world from a corporate standpoint, and I could see my path to success. Then in 2008, GM's bankruptcy started to come around since we had fallen off from a financial standpoint and run into some financial issues. I looked around to my bosses and my colleagues, and there was an abundant amount of fear."

As he began to look closer at his bosses, one of them was transferred to Shanghai from California with teenage kids. One was forced into early retirement, and another one got demoted! "I started to look like, man, these people don't have power over their careers or even where they live! You work so hard for these opportunities and for someone else to be able to take them away. Sometimes it's politics; sometimes we just get pushed out because we're not someone's guy or gal. If they just don't like you or you're too close to someone else, then that could be a wrap for you! You must keep these things in mind since sometimes it's not really about how good you are or how hard you work. You have to figure out how to create other streams of income, so you can continue to take care of your family and make decisions that are best for you and your family."

John's experience is very similar to many others working in private industry. You work hard for a company and give it your all, only to be a number when it's time to cut the cost to give shareholders a return. Many workers today just simply don't like their career or job, and it has gotten to a point where it becomes stressful and harmful for their health. On the opposite side of the coin, some people love what they do for a living every day and wake up each day excited to go work a job that's aligned with their passions and gifts. Work becomes a source of energy instead of a burden when you operate in this space and use your God-given gift(s) daily.

Regardless of which side of the corporate-versus-entrepreneur debate you belong to, both must make the leap in becoming savvy investors to get their money working for them so they aren't forced to trade their time for money indefinitely. Because at the end of the day, money is simply a tool we can leverage. Some people want more money to buy a bigger house, fancy car, shiny jewelry, or other luxuries. However, for most successful real estate investors whose stories I captured in this book, including me, the motivation for investing in real estate is to obtain freedom. Freedom from having to trade time for money and the ability to live a life where your schedule is based on your desires and priorities and not the need to pay bills.

NO MORE LAYOFFS
To continue to hit home the point of how having a misalignment of goals and values with your employer can be a real issue, I want to share the story of my friend, Jerome Myers. Jerome is a phenomenal full-time multifamily investor who

walked away from a six-figure job in an organization he helped build from its infancy. He started in corporate America as a structural engineer, got on the leadership track, and received a lot of training and exposure. From there, he worked in a couple of consulting firms before he landed his last job in corporate America, where he built a twenty-million-dollar business for a division of a construction company.

"It was super exciting because I was employee number two in that division, responsible for profit and loss and everything else. Over eight months, we led the business from two employees, up to 150, with twenty million dollars in revenue that year and a 30 percent profit margin. But what rubbed me the wrong way is that we had to cut the workforce in half at the end of that year! With that big profit, I didn't understand why people needed to be on the street trying to figure out how they would pay for holiday gifts or pay their mortgage next month. So, I went another year, and we had another successful year in business, and then we went through the same thing again. I said I can't do this."

Fortunately, he had been fiscally fit for a long time. He was able to top $100,000 in income when he was only twenty-six, and he chose not to grow his lifestyle to go with the income. "I was able to put money away, and I put money away aggressively, so when I walked out the door, I had a little over a year's worth of savings. If I could do it all over again, I'd probably have two because it always takes longer than what you expect. And even today, I don't make the same money I made when I was in corporate America. I made a lot of money when I was in corporate America, but I don't need all of that to live. I've given up some income, but I've gained a ton of freedom! It's a balance, and for years, I said, I can't take this pay cut and go to something else because I wanted to be an entrepreneur. I've got two daughters, and I wanted something that if they didn't want to go work for somebody else, they could walk into and run. For me, it's about generational wealth and actually owning something and not just about real estate."

During his last corporate job, he had three different supervisors over the course of eighteen months, and he only interfaced with them every other week with face-to-face meetings only once a quarter with every other decision being his. He received the opportunity to be an entrepreneur running the business how he chose. So, the next logical step for him was to take the pay cut and build his own business since that six million dollars in profit the company made only earned him a $30,000 bonus. On top of that, his supervisor had the audacity to tell him he was overpaid! At the end of the day, he took those necessary baby steps to get to where he was ready to make the transition.

If you can save enough capital to cover expenses, you have the freedom to do whatever you think you want to do and turn it into a way to generate revenue. Of course, you don't have to leave your job unless it works for your situation. I knew I could do more by creating a family business with my wife to build our real estate portfolio, but I kept my job because I love serving in the Air Force. Your situation will be different, but the same principles apply. Jerome now leads his own company, The Myers Development Group, where he has built a multi-million-dollar portfolio and continues to provide passive investing opportunities for his investors. He also educates new multifamily investors via Myers Methods, his real estate education company.

IMPLEMENTATION

Many Americans today have a perception of security and safety in a job because they will get a paycheck every week or two. However, it's not guaranteed, not even if you're a government employee, so you never really know if this check will be your last. At some point, you must decide to take back control and bet on yourself. It won't be easy, but it will be well worth it. I always like to say you must become comfortable being uncomfortable! However, if you purposely seek out knowledge and network with other like-minded individuals, it will all work out. In the end, you will be glad you made those sacrifices to create generational wealth for your family.

Clearly, you are on the right path by simply taking the time to pick up this book to advance your real estate investing knowledge. Be encouraged since you aren't the first person to wander down the real estate investing path. I am a true believer that success leaves clues if we are wise enough to look for them. We live in a far-from-perfect society, but I can tell you from my experience visiting and working in more than a dozen countries around the world that no other country comes close to matching the opportunities to advance yourself and build real estate wealth from nothing as in America.

As we wrap up this chapter, we highlighted the disturbing trends between Americans today and their money. Fortunately, where we start in life isn't necessarily where we will end. I shared my personal story of evolving my definition of success over time as well as the story of two full-time real estate investors who left the clinching grasp of corporate America.

Let's take an opportunity to focus on you and your success. What is the number one myth about money you were taught growing up? Has it evolved at all? Another question to help you gain clarity is determining your unique talent or idea that can drive you to success. We all have gifts and abilities to bless this world with, but it can take faith to move past our fears and limiting beliefs. Taking those answers into account, what's the most important challenge you must overcome to accelerate your real estate investing journey?

CHAPTER 2

TODAY'S SUCCESSFUL MILLIONAIRE

───

*"You have to make the shift from being a consumer
in the economy to becoming an owner, and
you do it by becoming an investor."*

TONY ROBBINS

FROM $7 TO $250M+ APARTMENT PORTFOLIO

I was first introduced to Vinney Chipora in fall 2018 at a multifamily investor conference in Orlando, Florida. Professional conferences are an excellent opportunity to gain and share new ideas, learn about the latest industry innovations and trends, and provide an opportunity to network with other like-minded individuals. This was my first multifamily conference, and hundreds of people attended the event! There were two full days of guest speakers, and Vinney sat on an expert panel, giving insight on the future of the multifamily industry. He vividly discussed his humble journey of immigrating to the United States almost thirty years ago with basically no money to having a nine-figure real estate portfolio comprised of thousands of apartment units across the United States! I was intrigued by his story. I reached out to Vinney to learn more about him and how he achieved his success in real estate. I was fortunate enough to have the opportunity to sit down with him for thirty minutes and learn more about his story.

He grew up with six siblings in a one-bedroom apartment, never having a television, telephone, refrigerator, or a car—just a single bicycle. However, he was smart and resilient. He completed his bachelor's degree in mechanical engineering after receiving a merit scholarship to go to college since he was in the top 3 percent of his graduating class. I learned in India the government finds the top students and pays for their education, including tuition allowance every month, along with books. He received his big break when he received the opportunity to continue his education in the United States.

In December of 1975, at the age of twenty-two, he moved to Maryland with his uncle and aunt with only seven dollars to his name! Luckily, in his culture, they do not charge one another for housing or food, which helped him tremendously. "After my first semester, a friend asked me if I would like to sell books. This opportunity changed my life. I started knocking on doors working eighty hours a week. We would start working at 8 a.m. with my friend dropping me off until 9:30 p.m. when he returned to pick me up every day for six days a week. My dad already instilled in me the value of hard work, but selling books taught me how to take rejection with having doors slammed in my face. It taught me perseverance, confidence, and the power of working hard." As a real estate investor, you will have your share of adversity you will have to overcome. Whether it's making six hundred phone calls before finding someone interested in selling a discounted property or finding termite damage when you tear down a wall during renovation, real estate investing is all about meeting challenges head-on and persevering. Becoming successful takes effort and work; if it were easy, everyone would be successful in life.

Hard work is part of the equation for accomplishing anything that matters in life, whether it's investing in real estate or accomplishing a military mission. As a young captain in Afghanistan, I can remember leading a team of intelligence professionals working twelve or more hours a day for six months straight! It's what the moment called for, and our team was up to the task of supporting those units outside the wire, engaging the enemy, and putting their lives on the line day in and day out. If we didn't bring our A-game on a daily basis, lives could be unnecessarily put in danger. Unfortunately, in life, people fail to realize the sacrifices required to accomplish goals.

After obtaining his master's from Georgetown University, Vinney relocated to San Francisco and started working as a promotional consultant where he started his journey as a public speaker. He grew to become a major stockholder in the company until his retirement in 2015 after serving over thirty-seven years! Along the way, Vinney found a passion for real estate after encouragement from friends after he moved to California. They started buying in Texas, Georgia, and Reno, Nevada. After investing off and on for many years, in 2005, he obtained his broker's license and pivoted to commercial real estate.

After selling all their single-family rentals and moving full force into multifamily, Vinney has been a critical principal in acquiring over 4,500 apartment units across thirty-four syndications in the last ten-plus years. "I have raised over $147 million so far. Now, I can raise six to ten million dollars in only two to three days because our investor network has gone from none twelve years ago to nearly four hundred investors. My investors have given me millions of dollars because I have doubled, tripled, and even quadrupled their money." Success breeds success. In multifamily, we call it the law of the first deal. After "getting over the hump" of closing on your first deal, most investors build momentum and secure their next property, thus providing an opportunity for new investor partnerships in a short amount of time.

There's not a more humbling feeling than having someone invest their hard-earned money in a real estate project led by *you*. It's one thing to invest your money in your own deal, but the stakes become that much higher when you bring in investor partners. Our first investor was a relative we were very close to who was aware of the deals we were doing before we started sharing more on social media. For any active investor who has been around long enough, you learn that you can only go so far using your personal capital. Leveraging joint partnerships and bringing on limited partners allows like-minded investors to grow and diversify their portfolios while assisting you in growing yours at the same time.

As I wrapped up my conversation with Vinney, he went on to share more about what's possible when you put your investors first. He shared how one of his very first investors, from over twelve years back, still invests with him and has invested $3.8 million to date. Since that initial investment, the same individual has told multiple family members and in-laws about his experience to the point now this single investor has been responsible for close to twenty-eight million dollars invested with Vinney from a single referral. Taking care of investors is his number-one motto, an ethos every investor should live by.

Vinney's story was inspiring and unique. As you will see in the other stories shared in this chapter and the rest of the book, you can pick up certain habits and traits that will significantly increase your ability to be successful at whatever you set your mind to. Success is a mindset. As I mentioned in the introduction, success is achieved through a plan that is 80 percent psychological and 20 percent skills.

MY MILLIONAIRE REAL ESTATE INVESTOR JOURNEY

In 2017, Fidelity performed a survey of investors with a net worth of over one million dollars. From Fidelity's research, they found that 88 percent of millionaires are self-made. The benchmark for most individuals is to achieve a net worth of a million dollars. For anyone who may not know, your net worth is simply the value of your assets minus your liabilities. I can remember when I first started working and setting that same one-million-dollar goal. You hear the stories of successful people who were millionaires, but I never really knew how they got there. In my case, I didn't know one single millionaire and had no clue how to build wealth. I had no strategy and almost thirty thousand dollars in debt as soon as I started my first job and nothing but uninformed assumptions when it came to achieving wealth.

I became fascinated with real estate after realizing I could buy a house, rent it out, and have someone pay my mortgage and still have money left over every month to put in my pocket. On top of that, I loved that it helped reduce my tax burden and eventually it would appreciate in value over time. I joined my local Real Estate Investor Association (REIA) fifteen miles north of my house in Macon, Georgia. I also latched on to a family friend, Alfred Grooms, who lived in Atlanta and owned his own financial consulting firm. He taught me how stocks worked, how to evaluate businesses and how money worked! Most don't know, but I was extremely close to leaving the Air Force after my original four-year commitment. We all know 2006 and 2007 were great, but after the recession fully hit in 2008, the entire economic landscape changed. Plus, I was offered my number-one job choice for my next assignment, making it a relatively easy decision to stay.

My second home acquisition happened in January 2011; soon after Melissa and I were married, I relocated to Newport News, Virginia, for my next Air Force assignment. We found a HUD foreclosure in great shape and located in a great golf community. We purchased the house for $208,000 using my VA loan again with no money down! We would rent the place out upon leaving for our next duty station, bringing in an extra $500 a month of cashflow. In July 2013, we were relocated to Northern Virginia where we purchased another HUD foreclosure. I knew from the last house that I had enough VA entitlement since I was moving into a more expensive area where the purchase limit was increased. VA loan entitlement is the dollar amount the Department of Veterans Affairs will guarantee on each VA home loan and helps determine how much a veteran can borrow before needing a down payment.

VA loan entitlement is typically either $36,000 or 25 percent of the loan amount up to the conforming loan limit. I found the house on the HUD website, and our realtor went the same day and shot a video and showed us the inside; we put a full-price offer at $280,000, and it was accepted. I saw it sold in 2007 for $390,000, and it didn't need any repairs, so it was a no-brainer!

During this assignment, our real estate investing business took off. In 2014, we bought our first rental property on Ave K in Birmingham, Alabama, sight unseen for $25,000 with monthly rent at $750. Next, we purchased another foreclosure at an online auction on 2nd Avenue in Birmingham for $6,700, sight unseen. The renovation cost us about $16,000, and we rented it out for $800 a month. We kept both of those through early 2015 until we sold them to fund our first flip project in Alexandria, Virginia. We learned an enormous amount about construction and remodeling on that project. To this day, our first flip was by far our most expensive and intense.

After it sold, we moved our operation virtual and started flipping houses in Birmingham, Alabama, due to the lower purchase prices, cost of materials, and labor. We went on to complete four more projects over the next two years. I would get a property under contract and then make the ten-hour drive down to Birmingham and get contractor bids to set our execution plan and set us up for success. At this point, I was extremely committed to the process and making it happen. I learned about projecting cashflows and carrying costs quickly after taking on two projects simultaneously. One of our Birmingham projects we held for nine months through a winter real estate cycle with a $60,000 repair budget and $2,200 monthly interest-only payments. It almost broke us, but it didn't. It helped us find our niche, buying homes more affordable to middle-class buyers and with lower carrying costs.

My next assignment took our real estate journey to the next level. We relocated to Panama City, Florida, in July 2017 and purchased another HUD foreclosure for $198,000. We spent about $25,000 to remodel it. A year later, it would appraise for $320,000. During that one-year time frame, I was hit with a six-month deployment overseas from March to September 2018. This prevented us from moving forward with any flip projects for over a year. However, I was still able to market and wholesale some deals before I left home. Three weeks before leaving, we found out Melissa was pregnant with our third child. Three weeks after returning home from that deployment, the Panama City area was devastated by a category five storm, Hurricane Michael, which displaced our family for six months. However, the adversity we faced wasn't a setback but a setup!

Overnight, there became tens of thousands of dilapidated homes. We put a crew together that is still with us today, and in 2019, we completed a total of nine projects. In 2020, in the middle of a pandemic, we completed four projects, including purchasing our first apartment building, an eighteen-unit property. We relocated back to Northern Virginia in November 2020 and bought another foreclosure with a VA loan. We still have our renovation business in Panama City and are on track to complete over a dozen projects for 2021. My real estate investing has been part time while I was still working full time, active duty and kicking ass. By 2021, our real estate portfolio has eclipsed $5 million with over $1.5 million in equity.

Millionaires are disciplined and willing to put in the work. As mentioned earlier, 88 percent are first-generation millionaires. Over the last two centuries, 90 percent of the world's millionaires have been created by investing in real estate. Some will tell you the only way you can become a millionaire is to stop buying five-dollar Starbucks coffee, not go to restaurants for dinner, and save as much as you can to invest in the stock market with your IRA/401K. I don't believe you would be reading this book if you wanted to sign up for that school of thought. You must have an abundance mindset and focus on creating more income, so you can afford to buy a five-dollar cup of coffee or buy anything else that makes you and your family happy. Real estate allows you to build a portfolio that produces passive cashflow that affords you the freedom to eventually not have to trade your time for money and allows your investments to pay for your lifestyle. It's not going to happen overnight, but I always say pay the price today so you can pay any price tomorrow.

HOW TO LOSE $50M AND STILL BOUNCE BACK

I had the pleasure of sitting down one-on-one with another successful real estate investor, Mr. Rod Khleif. Rod is an entrepreneur, real estate investor, and serial business owner who is passionate about business, life, success, and giving back. Rod has personally owned and managed over two thousand properties during his investing career. Rod is a no-nonsense guy who is extremely passionate about assisting others on their journeys as real estate investors. This became apparent as soon as our thirty-minute meeting started, and he began to share his thoughts and philosophy on finding success in life.

Rod started off reflecting on his childhood and immigrating to the United States. "When I was six, my mother, brother, and I emigrated from Holland. She moved us to Denver, and we lived quite poor. Mom was a live-in housemaid for a man and babysat on the side. But she bought the house across the street with babysitting money." Fortunately, his mom made a $20,000 profit selling their home in only three years. Seeing how this transaction played out inspired him to go into real estate at the young age of eighteen. Over the next twenty years, he would amass a fifty-million-dollar real estate fortune: eight hundred homes, multiple apartment complexes, and a beautiful beachfront mansion. Rod took a break and found a few pictures of his luxurious beachfront mansion to share with me as he reflected on that time in his life.

Rod continued and reflected on his childhood. "Immigrating was hard for me. I didn't speak English, and my mom, being the proud Dutch woman that she is, would send me to school in leather shorts and wooden shoes from Holland. It goes without saying that I'd get beat up a lot. And when bullies chased me home from school, my mother chased them off with a fly swatter, so I'd get beat up and ridiculed the next day all over again. So, my whole adult life, I'd done everything to prove to the world that I'm good enough. I'd been totally focused on myself." A lot of people have a self-centered mindset when it comes to building wealth. However, most wealthy people are active philanthropists and dedicate large amounts of their time and money to passionate causes. Rod created a foundation called Tiny Hands, fed seventy-five thousand children for the holidays, and gave tens of thousands of backpacks filled with school supplies.

"I lost everything in the market crash in 2008; fifty million dollars in real estate. I lost the beach-front mansion, my Mercedes...all the stuff that ultimately doesn't matter but that is quite painful to lose. I'd made the mistake of buying single-family homes to hold long term and cross collateralize them with my multifamily properties. The multifamily properties did fine, but the single-family homes pulled my entire portfolio down. But the opportunity in the crisis was a key lesson learned. Shortly after, he started his own podcast and began sharing those lessons learned thus far on his journey. He did hundreds of episodes, eventually hit a million downloads, and expanded it into a purpose-driven multi-million-dollar enterprise helping others succeed in real estate.

We continued to speak in greater detail on what he felt led to his overall success and some of the traits of other millionaires he engages with. Many of these traits and principles are covered in greater detail later in the book. The first step is defining your goals and vision for what you want from your life. In the classic *Think and Grow Rich*, Napoleon Hill wrote about finding your burning desire, so when you are faced with adversity or get knocked down, you have exactly what you need to get up and bounce back. The second step is to make a decision or a commitment to what you want. The Latin root word for decide is cut off. At this point, you are no longer just interested; now, you are committed to doing whatever it takes to achieve your goals. Eric Thomas says,

"You have to want it as bad as you want to breathe." Rod told me, "Motivation will get you started; commitment will bring you home."

The third step comes down to faith. You must believe good is going to happen to you. You can't get caught up in the negative, whether it's in the latest news topic, online gossip blogs, or other people in your life. Lastly, you must stay laser-focused on your goals in life. Rod shared an example in his life when his efforts weren't streamlined and focused. "I remember when I used to have so many businesses going at the same time, two frozen yogurt shops, a few vending carts selling ice cream bars, a card printing business, and I was doing real estate. Everything suffered because my focus was diluted; I got rid of everything except for the real estate, and I bought five hundred houses in that run."

Today, Rod continues to build successful businesses and add value to people's lives. As one of the nation's top real estate trainers, he has personally owned and managed over two thousand properties. He still hosts his "Lifetime Cash Flow Through Real Estate Investing" podcast, which has been downloaded over ten million times! Also, he still directs his Tiny Hands Foundation, which has helped more than one hundred thousand community kids and families in need.

IMPLEMENTATION
Right now, as you are reading this page, you have everything you need to achieve success in real estate investing and become a millionaire. However, it requires you to commit to the process and put aside any doubts and limiting beliefs.

We all have naysayers and people who don't believe in us or our dreams, whether they are malicious or just trying to save us from failure. I'm here to tell you that you will fail at some point along the way, but it's all about how you decide to use the failure. Will you view it as a negative moment and not take away any substance or life lessons from it, or will you view it as a seminar giving you the necessary knowledge to grow you into the savvy investor you aspire to be? You can't have a testimony without first going through the test!

As you aim to move forward on your millionaire journey, you will need to understand where you have come from and where you are headed. I shared my story of how I built my million-dollar portfolio over a fifteen-year span. What has been your number one limiting belief holding you back from doing more as a real estate investor? It is imperative to immediately start focusing on changes you can make today. What has been the largest hurdle you have overcome on your real estate investing journey? Was it tough to move past it? I shared the motivating story of how Vinney came to the US with only seven dollars before embarking on a journey to build a nine-figure multifamily portfolio. Furthermore, I discussed how Rod bounced back from losing fifty million dollars to gain it all back while building an education company and charity along the way. Over the course of the next week, I encourage you to make a list of all your assets and liabilities so you can calculate your net worth and assess where you are today. Just remember, if those other investors and I can do it, you certainly can too!

CHAPTER 3

LAW OF THE FIRST DEAL

———

"Twenty years from now, you will be more disappointed by the things that you didn't do than by the ones you did do."

MARK TWAIN

It's challenging to implement significant, strategic change whether in your life or a major corporation. Newton's First Law of Motion states that an object in motion tends to stay in motion, and an object at rest will stay at rest unless the object is acted upon by an outside force. It takes considerable energy to get started and to make continual, sustained progress in any area of life. Real estate investing is no different, as your first deal is usually the toughest. Many real estate investors refer to it as "The Law of the First Deal." The ability to gain the hands-on experience of the first deal is critical to break down any limiting beliefs or doubts you may have in your ability to become a successful real estate investor. I know a phenomenal military spouse and real estate investor who started her journey with their first single-family home purchase to live in and transitioned it to a rental.

OVERNIGHT LANDLORD TO PRIVATE LENDER

For many Americans, their first real estate deal is the purchase of their primary residence. It's not an investment per se since you're living in it, but the future transition to a rental property can set a solid path for your real estate investing future when done properly. You can leverage low down payment government programs through the VA and FHA to buy the property. Additionally, you can buy a foreclosure to secure instant equity or purchase a multi-unit property with one, two, or three residents paying rent while you live in the other unit.

Over time, you can save additional capital to purchase your next property whether it's one year (VA/FHA minimum occupancy timeframe) or a few years later. Your investing journey is a marathon, and it starts with your first deal! Let's look at a few real estate investors and see how they got started on their real estate investing journey.

I met Alex Breshears through a mutual associate who introduced us. We hopped on a video call to chat about her real estate investing experience. Alex has a phenomenal story that includes moving around with the Navy and living at nineteen different addresses in only a twenty-year time frame. Alex and her husband were stationed at some places for as little as three months, six months, nine months, the longest being twenty-two months at their current station in Virginia.

They started their investing journey over twenty years ago. She started, "We bought our first home, a little, quaint townhouse in Jacksonville, Florida, using our VA loan. We moved out of that about two years later to a larger house that we purchased with conventional financing in a nice neighborhood where we wanted to live. Soon after, we would PCS, or relocate for non-military people, and rent it out like the first one to bring in more passive income." This was great for them, but no one prepared them for being a landlord after relocating across the country. They didn't research and fully digest all the subtle requirements of being a landlord and the skills needed to be successful.

She continued, "We never had a conversation with someone about being a remote landlord even if you have a property manager, which we did. Our townhouse was a middle unit. So, you're sharing a large structure with multiple units. So, we had an issue with the neighbor's house because they needed a new roof, and it caused a dreadful leak into our wall. In Florida, with the humidity, it caused a concerning mold problem, but because the true source of the leak was the neighbor's roof, there was very little that could be done. It takes grit to be a landlord or a real estate investor in general. There will always be unknown challenges/issues that will need to be addressed."

Remote real estate investing really wasn't an option for them after this landlord experience. They were bouncing around a lot, so they weren't doing any active real estate investing for many years because they had the mindset of not wanting to invest remotely since they absolutely hated being a landlord. Fortunately for them, they got back into investing. They were able to do a couple of fix-and-flips as partners with some associates. They brought the capital to the deal, and their partner dealt with the contractors and everything else. This brought them into the world of private lending.

Private lending has been instrumental in the growth of our home renovation company, Operation Restore LLC. I refer to my private lenders as partners since I value their relationship and the opportunity to assist them in continuing to build wealth in their portfolio. I will discuss private lending in greater detail when we get to chapter 8, which focuses on financing real estate deals.

Pre-COVID, Alex and her husband completed some private lending off and on throughout the years. When COVID hit a lot of hard money lenders, lenders abruptly quit lending, leaving many real estate investors with no funding solution. Ultimately, the pandemic empowered them into a new level of investing!

She went on to share the details. "There was an active-duty service member that we're friends with here in Norfolk, and we all were in a meetup via Zoom. He began talking about how he was going to lose out on this deal because the closing was in four days and his lender literally shut their doors that morning and told him they were going to take a break and weren't funding any more deals. So, I asked him to tell me about the deal. He shared the numbers, and I thought this was the exact type of property I'd want to lend on and the type of borrower I wanted to work with.

"I gave him my number, so we could talk offline and see if we could make it work. I met him two days later to walk and look at the property, and I agreed to fund him. I asked him if he could give me two weeks to have our attorney get all the paperwork and LLC needed to get the project up and running legally. He went back to the seller to ask for more time and ended up with a better deal. The seller ended up saying yes and carried the mortgage for a few months, subject to their existing financing.

This allowed us to only provide gap funding for renovations and holding costs until the property was sold."

After that project, the Breshears have been private lending ever since. It allows them the opportunity to work with other service members as all their borrowers have been active-duty service members or veterans. One significant clause or requirement to be approved for their funding is for the borrower to hire one active-duty service member, veteran, or military spouse during renovations because they genuinely believe in furthering and supporting the military community. This type of forward-thinking and leadership goes a long way in supporting the 1 percent of Americans who decided to take an oath to defend the United States of America, thus allowing the American Dream to even become a possibility.

MY FIRST RENTAL

My first rental came by way of me having to relocate due to my job. It wasn't a big shocker for me since moving every few years is part of the job. I always tell my mentees to start with the end in mind because you make money in real estate when you buy, not when you sell. It's always a good idea to have multiple exit strategies in case anything changes with your plan. The real estate agent's broker who sold me my home also had a property management company, so I decided to leverage them to manage my property once I left town. My place was originally built in 2003 and was new and lightly used since I lived alone and took care of the place. It has worked out well over the last eleven years, with me changing property managers only once and only having a total of two tenants over the same period.

As I reflect on my real estate journey, buying my first house and becoming a landlord gave me a tremendous amount of confidence. I still had student loans to pay back then, and I was helping my sister get through college. Thankfully, as a veteran, I could pay no money down and receive a little over $300 back at closing after seller closing cost assistance! Don't wait to buy real estate; buy real estate and wait!

I first ran across the idea of Law of the First Deal when I attended a multifamily event led by Michael Blank back in 2020. He also discussed it in detail in his book *Financial Freedom with Real Estate Investing*. Essentially, when you take action, you will build momentum in the right direction. This momentum follows you into your subsequent deals, which empowers you and makes the process less daunting. Multinational productivity coach Kirstin O'Donovan says, "Actions create habits that lead to success." A recent study by Gail Mathews, a psychologist from the Dominican University of California, found that those who set actionable tasks for their goals and leverage weekly progress reporting to peers tend to achieve 40 percent more than those who don't. To get the first deal done, you must get off the sidelines and take action! We will take a deeper look at goal setting in a future chapter.

ACTIVE-DUTY MARINE TO FULL-TIME MULTIFAMILY INVESTOR

I'm not the only real estate investor who picked up real estate investing after already starting a career. Meet Mr. Brian Briscoe, retired lieutenant colonel. He is an accomplished Marine officer who came from humble beginnings. He and

I sat down for our interview on a nice cool spring Saturday morning as he prepared to speak at the Mid-Atlantic Multi-family Conference later that day.

"When I was growing up, my dad was a letter carrier for the post office, and I have two older brothers, two younger brothers, and two younger sisters. His base salary in the 1980s was in the high $20,000s to low $30,000s range. So, it wasn't a lot of fun. He started working at the post office after I was born. I was raised with my dad, having spent almost my entire life working in the post office, and he would always tell me that I could do better! A better job and better education. So, growing up, my idea of success was a higher paying job than my dad because that's what he told me I needed to do. He encouraged me to get good grades because everything depended on getting good grades in high school to receive a scholarship in college."

Brian commissioned and started his career in the Marines. "I started making money. Instead of being a poor college student, I started making some real money. And I remember as a captain, it's the 2006 timeframe, and I was probably making $80,000 to $90,000. And the idea of going back to school for five years, just so I could become a college professor with a starting salary at $60,000 and ten years later begin making $100,000. It didn't make sense. I liked what I did for the military, it was very popular, and everybody thanks you for your service. At this point of time, I'm a captain or a major in the Marine Corps, but I started looking at success, as the next rank or becoming a commanding officer, and so I started chasing it!"

Brian went on to tell me there have only been two general officers from his career field in the history of the Marine

Corps. He started to see a glass ceiling at the rank of colonel. His definition of success was to make it to the rank of colonel, have a thirty-year career, and retire with a 75 percent pension. He was picking up real estate along the way to build his portfolio to build up his passive income, so at age fifty-five, he would retire as a full bird colonel.

His story is no different than a lot of ours. We look around at other people in our circles, do some research, and get a couple of degrees to set us up for success in our job of choice. We start our careers, get married, buy a house, a car, get a management position, have a couple of kids, and next thing you know, we are trying to figure out how we will retire. The pseudo-American Dream! However, Brian wasn't 100 percent sold on his definition of success after selling one of his early rental properties in which he walked away with over $140,000. When compared to his stock market investments through the DoD Thrift Savings Plan and everything else he invested, the return on selling the rental was off the charts, so he started thinking about how he could scale this newfound model.

For Brian, one of the most pivotal moments was on a Navy ship in the Gulf of Aden. He recalled hitting a super low point! "I was probably a little bit depressed. I may have been in an eight-by-twelve-foot room that I shared with one other guy with barely enough room for the two of us to be moving around at the same time. I was relatively isolated just because of my rank. I couldn't hang out with the Marines, and there were only a couple of majors on the ship, and they all had different jobs and different schedules. I don't quite remember if it was a birthday or what, but I remember just having a feeling that I can't keep doing this. I can't keep missing family events, and I can't keep missing birthdays, Christmas, Halloween, and everything else that comes along with it." At that point, that's when he realized his version of success wasn't going to work because of the negative effects on his family.

Success changes and evolves as we obtain wisdom and grow in life. Change is inevitable. I always tell those I coach; they must become comfortable being uncomfortable. We don't know it all, and we must have the courage to adjust our approach once we are presented with new facts that impact our reality. If we do nothing, we continue down the same path and reap the same results. After being presented with the fork in the road, Brian embraced change and started looking more in-depth into real estate, including multifamily, listening to the podcasts, and reading more books. In 2018, he went to his first big real estate investor conference and started seeing people who replaced their active income in two to three years, ultimately validating what he already knew.

His journey started to accelerate after networking and meeting Daniel Woodford, a retired Air Force officer. He heard him on a podcast as he was running across the bridge that connects Arlington, Virginia, to Washington, DC. "After running across that bridge and listening to an episode of Michael Blank's podcast where Daniel was a guest, his story was just like mine. He moved to the Pentagon, he wanted to get out and was tired of the military, and he started doing real estate full time and on nights and weekends while he was working in the Pentagon; he built up his portfolio. That's totally what I want to do!"

Brian went on to tell me how he stopped and, with sweaty fingers in the middle of August, tried to type out an email to him. With that inspiration, he had a new version of success, one where he had three years remaining at the Pentagon to reach twenty years of service and eligibility to retire. Upon retirement, he needed to replace his active-duty income by October 31, 2021. Ultimately, his new success goal affords him the ability to work when he wants and where he wants. I'm happy to share that Brian accomplished his goal in less than three years.

He replaced his active-duty income and will make more money in 2021 from multifamily than he will make from serving in the Marines. Now he's moving on to his next goal and a new version of success with him continuing to run his multifamily investment firm, Four Oaks Capital, and eventually hiring more staff and turning that active income into 100 percent passive income so he can have the freedom to be wherever he wants, whenever he wants.

SINGLE FAMILY RENTALS TO FINANCIAL FREEDOM

One last great success story that shows the power of getting your first deal is Mandy McAllister. I met Mandy after reaching out to her after seeing her story on Instagram. I started off our conversation by asking Mandy how her real estate journey got started. "You know, I always kind of had real estate in the back of my mind. I remember being nineteen years old at a party in Macon, Georgia, in college. It was at a friend's house, and I remember thinking, "How is she living in this house?" I recall being on the porch with her and she started explaining how her dad bought the house, and she rents out the rooms to her friends. I was like, "And you get to keep that money?" That's the best idea ever! So, this idea of real estate investing was something I wanted to do and had been in the back of my mind since my teens, but it wasn't until I dabbled with the learning piece for a very long time and until I became a mom in 2016. Three weeks before my kiddo was born, I bought my first property."

She started with a single-family, but soon after started looking at rentals. She told me, "I decided to take a bet on myself and fix and flip projects." That grew into doing more renovations and then keeping some using the "BRRRR" method: Buy, Renovate, Rent, Refinance, Repeat. Last year, they evolved and purchased their first apartment building. They have the same goal, but now realize they can leverage different vehicles to get them there faster. When she learned more about apartments, she realized it was a "Ferrari" to get her to the ultimate destination a lot faster.

If you learn the strategy of leveraging multifamily and some of the other commercial real estate vehicles, you can get where you want to go a whole lot faster. Mandy has her cash flow requirements from the retirement calculator she built to capture what she needed to be comfortable and to leave her job. Example: If I need $10,000 passive income every month to leave my job *comfortably*, and I'm currently getting $200 in rental income per door, I know I will need to acquire fifty single-family homes in fifty separate transactions. In contrast, I can acquire a 150-unit property that produces at least $200 per door in a single transaction. The math is the same. You can get non-recourse debt on these larger properties that you can't get on a single-family property. Non-recourse debt is a type of loan secured by collateral, which is usually property. If the borrower defaults, the issuer can seize the collateral but cannot seek out the borrower for any further compensation, even if the collateral does not cover the full value of the defaulted amount.

With Mandy's retirement calculator, she was able to reach her goal in June 2021. She is currently road mapping how to pay it forward. She started a group called Aspiring Women Achieving More, which is a true passion of hers. "It's really important that our female business leaders emulate lifting each other up and clapping loudly for each other. We have two arms for one reason: to support ourselves, but then to reach back and pull somebody else up. I have seen the reduction in stress, increase in fulfillment, and so many other benefits from just figuring the money stuff out, so I can go live my life. I'm here to preach the gospel to as many who will listen because it is quite literally life-changing."

IMPLEMENTATION
It should be apparent now that you must get started on your journey as a real estate investor. If the ordinary people whose stories I shared in this chapter and I were able to do it, you can too! The word "procrastination" is derived from the Latin verb *procrastinare*—to put off until tomorrow. When we procrastinate, we are extremely aware we're avoiding the task in question, but also that doing so is probably not a good idea. Yet we do it anyway.

Life is short, and tomorrow isn't promised to any of us! Your most challenging deal may or may not be your first deal. If you trust the process and follow the blueprint for success, you will be in an excellent position for long-term wealth. The book's next section will go into the habits and traits you will need to begin or take your real estate investing to the next level.

Ultimately, everyone's first deal will be different, yet each one will assist in building the necessary momentum to complete your next deal. Alex started, like me, with transitioning a personal residence to a rental upon relocating to a new duty location. What steps can you implement today to complete your first deal or to secure your next one? How will it make you feel to accomplish this goal? Both Brian and Mandy made the leap from single-family investing to full-time multifamily investing to scale their portfolios in a shorter amount of time to create enough passive income. Passive income will allow you the opportunity to eventually replace your W2 job. How will getting started in real estate investing improve your life? In the next chapter, we will learn the number-one habit of millionaire real estate investors and how to implement the law of the first deal.

CHAPTER 4

TAKE ACTION

"Do you want to know who you are? Don't Ask.
Act! Action will delineate and define you."

THOMAS JEFFERSON

Just as it is in life, every real estate investor's journey is different. However, every successful millionaire real estate investor, regardless of their asset class of choice, has one major trait in common. They took action. To be successful in real estate, you must take action and buy your first deal!

In today's information age, one has access to endless amounts of data at their fingertips for any topic of their choosing with an enormous amount being free. You can even access free college-level instruction from Ivy League schools such as Princeton and Harvard Universities. Additionally, podcasts provide unprecedented access to tactical-level experts from any and every industry. So, it is extremely easy for someone new to real estate investing to become overwhelmed with information as they listen to podcasts, watch YouTube, attend meetups, and read books. Analysis paralysis can set in very easily if you aren't careful. When coupled with fear, it can cause an impassable barrier in acting and making progress in obtaining your investing goals.

FROM WORKING THREE JOBS TO HAVING YOUR OWN TV SHOW

I want to share a great story from my friend Dave. Dave is one of the most down-to-earth, straight-shooting guys you will ever meet. Dave immigrated to the US at the age of nineteen from an impoverished inner-city neighborhood in London, England. After moving here and eventually becoming a firefighter and working odd jobs during the week, he mentally and physically entered a bad place. Some weeks, he would work 120 hours to provide for his family! Dave shared with me, "It's amazing. You get to a point where you're forced into making decisions sometimes, and I'm praying and praying my God help me. I was humbled. I said, 'Look, Lord, teach me, help me; I'm crying like a baby for real!' A commercial came on the radio in my truck, and it was for a real estate seminar about foreclosures, an hour and a half seminar for free."

The seed was planted. However, it didn't bear immediate fruit. He didn't go and attend the seminar. It took almost a year before he took action to become more educated on real estate. When he participated in the seminar, the instructor started saying things he'd never heard before. I could hear the excitement pick up in Dave's British accent. "The instructor asked, 'Are you sick and tired of being sick and tired and trading your time for somebody else's money, building their retirement, their legacy, taking care of their children's education, buying them a nice house, giving them a good night's sleep?' He said, 'Are you sick and frickin' tired of doing that? And if you are, you can do something different. If you choose to!' And for the first time in my life, I started looking at choices. And what I saw was that I could choose to learn a new way of thinking. I could choose to learn a new way of spending my time."

This was what he needed. When the student is ready, the teacher will appear. Dave started reconditioning his thinking. He started thinking about how he could get money to work for him instead of him working for money. He wanted to know how he could have his money working while he slept and how he could perform a job one time and have it pay him repeatedly. These are the fundamental philosophies behind real estate.

Let's get back to Dave's story. Dave exclaimed, "I was feeling absolutely fearless, and I doubted myself. Was it new? Was it uncomfortable? Yes, but I was freaking fearless because I was forced and beaten into submission. The old way of doing things wasn't working. I followed mentors and coaches, and I sought people out in my life who were positive, not negative. I was so committed to doing my first deal, which was a $5,000 wholesale transaction. I made $5,000 and didn't even own the house, and I'm like, *Holy crap, this feels illegal!* I can't wait for the cops to show up on my city block to lock me up. But I earned it, man. With my brain and my fortitude, I earned it. I did it; I went after it!"

As a result, Dave was recognized by the people leading the education program when another opportunity presented itself. This time the opportunity was a real estate flipping show. Initially, Dave's limited beliefs popped up as he asked what the hell the guy was thinking since he didn't even have a real business and he was still working out of the firehouse. However, he didn't walk away from the opportunity; he acted! He skimmed the plain, vanilla application, asking about his company and the other members of his team, etc. However, he thought outside of the box on how best to make himself stand out. He knew from being in the real estate education space that there were some heavy hitters out there, and he needed to separate himself from the pack if he wanted anybody to even think about giving him a TV show.

Dave, in his thick British accent, told me, "So I loaded my application with profanity... all the words my grandmother said I should never say! Go F@!& Yourself LLC was the name of my company, don't waste my time, blah blah blah. I mean, I really went at it. And look, New York called. I sent it in, and within fifteen minutes, I got a 212 area code calling my phone. And they said, 'You're either a lunatic or you're a genius.' I asked, 'What's the difference?' I told them to stop wasting my frickin' time, get on a plane, and let's go baby go! It's just been in motion ever since. I've always looked to level up." This Dave is none other than Dave Seymour, who starred in A&E's hit TV show, *Flipping Boston*.

Too often in life, we want to know how it all ends and what the prize is without truly embracing the journey or the process to get us there. Sometimes in life, it simply comes down to taking small actions and stepping out on faith to place us on the path to our destiny. It won't always be easy, and the road will be tough at times, but that's okay. Therefore, we chase our dreams and not the dreams of others because when you face adversity or setbacks, it becomes infinitely easier to keep the faith and overcome when you have a clear conviction on why failure isn't an option.

Sometimes, you must get sick and tired of being sick and tired and act. Tony Robbins, a world-renowned consultant and motivational speaker, encourages individuals seeking motivation to take action to examine their mood and evaluate their energy levels. A positive state of mind will empower optimism, and a negative state of mind can stifle progress. Eating right and exercising have a direct impact on your energy levels.

If you are looking to become successful in life, whether as a real estate investor, electrician, or any other profession in life, the one key is acting. There are plenty of sayings, analogies, and clichés used to convey just how important acting is. One individual I love listening to when it comes to success is comedian and *Family Feud* host Steve Harvey. I recently watched an interview with Steve on the *Sip and Smoke* TV series with Cam Newton, where he provided thoughts about success. He said, "You have to take the stairs; there is no elevator to success." I also recall from one of Steve's talk show episodes; he provided a great analogy comparing success to a parachute on someone's back standing at the edge of a cliff. To be successful, you must take action and jump. There is no chance of your parachute opening on the cliff. We must take the leap of faith and start living instead of simply existing!

HOW I SECURED MY FIRST FLIP
Webster defines action as the accomplishment of a thing, usually over a period, in stages, or with the possibility of repetition. One of the largest impediments to acting is analysis

paralysis. We have all been there before, and it's something everyone must move past. *Wall Street Journal* and national best-selling author Scott H. Young says analysis paralysis is a specific form of procrastination that convinces you that you haven't given something enough thought or performed enough research to move forward. However, he recommends removing the anxiety and fear of doing the thing you're avoiding. For me, I have learned over the years to focus on what I want to happen versus focusing on the fear of what might happen if I come up short. I'll share with you the time when I came to a crossroads in my life where I needed to act to receive my breakthrough.

In early spring 2015, I had finished negotiating a $200-million-plus contract extension for my software development contract. We were navigating an austere resource environment, which forced us to cut back our normal spending allocation as we advanced. Through those negotiations, my team was able to save more than ten million dollars over the next two years. I loved my job, my team, and the vote of confidence our leadership had given me. Leading diverse teams as an officer in the Air Force, both at home and abroad, requires calculated risk and taking decisive actions to accomplish the mission. It's a learned skill, and you become more comfortable the more you execute the skill. This new milestone on my program gave me an awakening sense of my innate ability to operate and deliver at a high level. I took this new level of confidence and embarked on our next journey, our first fix-and-flip project!

Melissa and I started our online search and purposefully searched for our first project. I knew we had to take massive action to reach our goal. I have learned it can take dozens of properties underwritten and offers made before obtaining a deal. We were scouring the internet daily, consistently searching our list of websites with deals. Also, we let our realtor, who sold us our current home at the time, know our buying criteria so she could send anything that looked promising our way. It didn't take long before we found the one—an upcoming auction for a bank foreclosure in Alexandria, Virginia.

Our realtor, Annabel, was originally from England and had a distinct accent my wife loved to hear. "Mr. Lynum," Annabel exclaimed, "this will need a lot of work, but for the right price, we can do it." Annabel was a house flipper as well, and I leaned on her experience and insight to get over my fear of potentially losing a lot of our savings and amassing more debt. Aligning yourself with others who are strong in the areas where you are weak is critical to success. As you flip houses and do more and more projects, you become less anxious and more confident in identifying issues with a home and estimating rehabs as well.

This was our first one, and it would be one of our most extensive rehabs to date. The house had been vacant for multiple years, which led to its rundown condition. The home was two levels with the kitchen, dining room, bedroom, bathroom, and washroom on the lower level with the living room, two additional bedrooms, and bathroom upstairs. The home had no power for some time, which caused the lower level to back up with water during heavy rains. This cycle repeated for years and ultimately created a black mold issue on the lower level, which would require remediation. The tax record said it had a pool as well. This was starting to become more than a small cosmetic rehab the more we learned.

I burned the bridge behind me, and I was all in. At first, I was concerned about my wife's buy-in, but she was the unwavering rock and motivational speaker who provided the encouragement I needed to tackle these challenges head-on. We had less than a week before the auction would start and for us to perform our due diligence and determine our max bid. With this being our first project, we had zero experience renovating a pool or remediating black mold. However, I did my research to bind our risk. Due to the mold issue, no one was permitted to enter the property. From the outside, everything looked reasonably well. It needed a new paint job, but the roof was fine.

However, when peering through the side window, you could see the mold and damage caused by water over the years. A mold remediation company had given me an estimate of $7,800 to remediate the lower-level base of the house dimensions. I tried to access the backyard, but the fence was locked. I had spoken with a cool pool repairman, Paul, to get an estimate for the pool work sight unseen. He was an immigrant from Bulgaria and had been in the pool business for over ten years, and he spoke English, Russian, and Bulgarian. Based on the pool dimensions, a complete update with replacing the perimeter tile line, copping bricks, and resurfacing the entire pool would be around $10,000. However, there was a catch. Paul told me, in his Bulgarian accent, "My friend, as long as there is water in the pool, you will be safe! If it doesn't have water in it, we can have some major problems."

Now, we were at the property. The mold problem had been summarized and fully understood, so the only thing that stood between us and the green light to buy this property was this rusted master lock dangling off the wooden fence. "Shoot! It's locked," I shouted. Melissa looked at me and said, "So, what are we going to do now?" I looked at her and, without any hesitation, said, "I'm going to jump the fence!" She looked at me with a slight smile mixed with a face of concern and asked me, "Are you serious?" I had no other options, and I had to know if the pool had water in it or not. The auction representative told us we could look around the property, and that's exactly what we did!

The fence was a standard six-foot privacy fence, and the house sat on a corner lot. I needed a running start, so I figured approaching from the front would be my easiest route since I already peeked over the fence and saw a raised brick flower bed on the other side. Melissa went back to our SUV to wait for me to take my leap into the backyard. I played basketball in high school and was still active and in good shape, so I knew I could clear the fence. I stood beside our SUV in the driveway and surveyed my surroundings before I took my leap of faith not only into the backyard but into my real estate investing business! It was all clear.

I took off as if I had been blasted out of the chamber of a rifle and headed toward the fence. After about eight steps, I leaped onto the top of the wooden fence and perched my torso oh so carefully on top of the fence, so I could slide down the backside. Once I landed in the flowerbed in the backyard, I grinned and congratulated myself on my act of bravery. I jumped out of the flower bed and made my way to the pool. The flowerbed and the grass in the yard were overgrown and knee-high. However, quite a bit of concrete around the pool and area led to the back porch of the house.

The pool had an enclosure made from two-by-fours and fence wire that covered the entire length of the pool. Underneath the doomsday-looking contraption was the blackest water I had ever seen in my life. I was elated as if I just won the lottery. We were in business! I took a couple of pictures and looked in the other windows before I hurried back over the fence to head home.

A couple more weeks went by, and I was extremely busy in the office, so the time flew. The auction wasn't a traditional auction, so we placed our proposed bid of $216,000 around lunchtime on April 28, 2015. Late that afternoon, I received an email from Jose, the regional sales manager for the auction company. He wanted to speak with me to discuss our offer. He confirmed our offer price and passed it to the bank for formal acceptance since we were the highest bidder. The next day around noon, we received an automated email from the auction company stating our offer had been accepted.

This was a milestone example of taking action to kick off our real estate flipping business. However, as an investor, you must become comfortable with change and acting daily—whether it's following up with potential sellers or analyzing properties to make offers on properties. You will probably never have all the information you need to make important decisions, but that's okay. With time, you will gain experience and confidence to lower your risk and increase your effectiveness in making those decisions and ultimately becoming an astute investor.

BUYING MY FIRST HOME
I recall the "Parable of the Talents" found in the Bible, Matthew 25:14-30, which tells a story of a master who was leaving on a journey. Before he departed on his journey, he turned

over his talents or property, to his servants based on their ability. This left one servant with five talents, another with three, and the last with one. Upon his return, the master asked each of his servants how they managed the talents in his absence. The first and second servants took advantage of the opportunity and increased the value of the talents entrusted to them. They were rewarded for acting and being good stewards of what they were given. Unfortunately, the third servant took a different approach and buried his talent out of fear. The master reprimanded him for being lazy and took his talent away. This parable speaks to the need to take action with the God-given abilities bestowed upon us. Everyone has different talents; however, each of us has exactly what we need to be successful in real estate and in every facet of our lives.

Faith is a critical component to acting and moving forward. I remember how scared and nervous I was about buying my first house. I lived in Warner Robins, Georgia, for just about a year after commissioning as a second lieutenant in the Air Force. One of my good friends, Nick Battle, found this duplex property for sale. Nick called me: "Hey Jay2, man, we gotta get this duplex I found, bro! I get one side, and you get the other side." I had never purchased anything in my name before since my parents gave me my first car, and I had just recently gotten my debt under control from my credit card bills I ran up in college.

When it comes to taking action, there is some psychology behind it. Starting out, you must consciously recognize you almost never feel like acting. We are programmed to feel good, and many times taking action makes us uncomfortable. The second step is to make room for discomfort. I like to call it getting comfortable being uncomfortable. If you struggle with being uncomfortable, you will struggle with taking action. Ultimately, you must decide the result, or your reason "why" is worth the temporary discomfort. From there, you simply must set a commitment and start. Did you know that responsibility was originally written as response-ability? By owning your inaction, you own your ability to respond. I'm here to tell you that you can't fail. There are no failures in life, only life lessons that make us wiser if we choose to learn from them.

I was hesitant at first, but the more I investigated it and got smart on the details, I became more and more comfortable. I realized I would save over $200 per month compared to what I was paying in rent for my apartment. My bank approved my application quickly with a 100 percent VA loan, and I received a $320 check at closing. After moving past the fear of the unknown and buying my first property, I was infatuated with real estate. Taking this single action led to a multi-million-dollar portfolio of thirty-plus units thus far and the opportunity to educate others on the power of real estate to create generational wealth.

IMPLEMENTATION
Before taking action as a real estate investor, I had consumed hundreds of hours of personal reading, podcasts, seminars, networking, and meetups before executing our first flip project. Starting out, my favorite podcasts were the "Biggerpockets" podcast and "The Real Estate Guys." As I looked to grow my flipping business, I found investors like Max Maxwell on

YouTube. There are levels to success, and there is no such thing as overnight success. At that moment in time, we had two solid rental properties we previously lived in, and they were performing great. Additionally, we purchased two investment properties that required renovation in the Birmingham, Alabama, market. We sold both of those to have cash reserves to take on a flip project in Northern Virginia. We all have the same amount of time every day, but it all comes down to how we choose to use our time.

If you focused on reading just ten pages a day about real estate, you would have read 3,650 pages or the equivalent of roughly thirteen books in one year. If you choose to commit to the journey and make a few small changes, I have faith you will realize the success in real estate you are seeking. Megachurch pastor Bishop TD Jakes says, "Your passion is your conviction about it, your purpose is why you do it, your destiny is where." Passion and purpose are joined at the hip and move together, lockstep, toward destiny. Where there is passion, connect it to your purpose. Then set your goals higher than you think humanly possible. You will find your reward."

Earlier in this chapter, I shared Dave Seymour's story of perseverance, and it demonstrated how good things can happen once we decide to act. This is one of the first principles I teach students in my mastermind group. Once you have the basics understood, the only objective left is to act and find your next deal.

Have you been suffering from analysis paralysis? During this chapter, I shared my experience leading to the purchase of my first fix-and-flip property, along with a quick synopsis of how I bought my very first house. I sometimes wonder how different my life would have been if I had never moved out in faith and committed to those actions. What life accomplishments are potentially awaiting you once you commit to moving forward and taking more action in real estate? I encourage you to commit to three actions this week to accelerate your real estate investing journey. In the next chapter, we will look at how to properly define goals to focus your actions on those tasks leading to your future success.

CHAPTER 5

GOAL SETTING

———

"If you're bored with life, you don't get up every morning with a burning desire to do things—you don't have enough goals."

LOU HOLTZ, AMERICAN FOOTBALL
PLAYER, COACH, HALL OF FAMER

I want to start this chapter with a brief story from the NBA Hall of Famer and billionaire Michael Jordan. Michael gave details on his approach to setting goals and the impact it had on his success in his book *I Can't Accept Not Trying: Michael Jordan on the Pursuit of Excellence.*

"I approach everything step by step....I had always set short-term goals. As I look back, each one of the steps or successes led to the next one. When I got cut from the varsity team as a sophomore in high school, I learned something. I knew I never wanted to feel that bad again...So I set a goal of becoming a starter on the varsity. That's what I focused on all summer. When I worked on my game, that's what I thought about. When it happened, I set another goal, a

GOAL SETTING · **73**

reasonable, manageable goal that I could realistically achieve if I worked hard enough. Take those small steps. Otherwise, you're opening yourself up to all kinds of frustration. Where would your confidence come from if the only measure of success was becoming a doctor? If you tried as hard as you could and didn't become a doctor, would that mean your whole life was a failure? Of course not. All those steps are like pieces of a puzzle. They all come together to form a picture…. Not everyone is going to be the greatest….But you can still be considered a success….Step by step, I can't see any other way of accomplishing anything."

If you equate the principle of building a new house, then goal setting is equivalent to the blueprints for the house. The blueprint lays out the interior space plan, sets a budget, and lays out the home's complete structure from the foundation to the interior room layout. Your goals lay out those objectives you set out to accomplish for your life, business, and real estate investing decisions. However, many people go through life feeling lost or adrift and never really see any substantial progress toward their dreams.

This helpless feeling is caused by not spending the necessary time to think about what they want out of life and formulating them into specific, measurable, actionable, relevant, and time-bound (SMART) goals. As a real estate investor, goal setting is extremely important to focus on those specific objectives necessary to meet your long-term passive income goals. I'll share with you the story of Spencer Hilligoss, who set strategic goals to leave his lucrative corporate job to become a full-time multifamily real estate investor.

GOAL SETTING TO LEAVE CORPORATE AMERICA

Spencer was a thirteen-year career technology leader in multiple software companies, with three of them considered unicorns with a billion-dollar valuation and up. He built a four-billion-dollar loan origination group at LendingHome, the number one fix and flip lender in the country. However, he was just a little bit of a round peg in a square hole in the businesses as he grew up in a real estate brokerage household where his dad was a broker for thirty years. Spencer would help him with open houses when he was as young as thirteen years old, but he didn't initially see himself working in the real estate space.

However, as Spencer advanced in his corporate career and sometimes worked eighty-plus hours a week, he found himself looking back on his family and wanting to spend more time with those he cared most about. For him to be able to spend more time with his family, he set some strategic goals along the way. "We set a big goal of being financially free in fifteen years, and we set that goal now six years ago, I think, give or take a few quarters, roughly; however, we decided after we put down the numbers on paper that was just too long!

"We chopped it down to seven years, and we said, let's go figure out how to get completely financially free, and I'm talking about fully passive, no active income whatsoever. It will cover a comfortable lifestyle, including family fun and entertainment. We don't want to go buy a jet, as I have no interest in that, but I want to be able to be a great dad and be a great present husband. So, the goal setting is key. It gets a lot of playtime for everyone out there who has already achieved success, and that's for a very good reason. Nothing else should be happening before the goal setting is complete, and you should be able to break down that goal." Spencer was able to break down their goals from one year to a quarter to a month down to daily goals. Aligning your daily actions with your goals is critical to holding yourself accountable and reaching your success.

You must have a plan and goals to get you where you want to be in life, and it won't always be easy and pretty. Spencer continued sharing his story and the first goal-setting session that Jennifer and he had throughout a full weekend. "There were tears, there was laughing, and there was reconciliation there; it was real. And if you're not goal setting, I'm not saying you must get into fights over it; it just means that if you're not having honest conversations about your integrated, full picture goals with your spouse or your fiancé or your better half, you're missing the mark. There's one set of goals integrated for life; they are not your professional goals and your personal goals. They are your life goals."

So many times in life, we act and boom; we experience a setback or small failure. In these times, we must return to our passion or our "why" so we don't completely stop and let adversity defeat us. Mike Tyson had a phenomenal quote about perseverance. He said, "Everyone has a plan until they get punched in the mouth." We all have plans and goals, but life happens. In the Air Force, we say, it's great to have a plan, but the enemy gets a vote. In these moments, I love to point back to my faith. If the Lord has kept me and brought me through all the situations, setbacks, storms, and hurdles I have faced to date, why would I lose hope now? It's imperative for us to be unwavering in our chase for our goals and create financial freedom. Our goals serve as a long-term vision and short-term motivation as we execute.

In the Air Force, we call goals our objectives that we need to meet to accomplish our mission. We start at the higher, strategic level to understand what success looks like. We further decompose those objectives to mid-tier operational level objectives bound in scenarios or actual operations. The last level resides at the tactical level. Here, tactical-level objectives are the tasks we need to complete to accomplish our operational-level objectives. Once we define what success in life means to us, our mission is set! From there, we decompose our strategic goals down to daily executable tasks.

SMART GOALS

George Doran wrote a great article back in 1981 detailing how corporate managers can write effective, SMART goals for the organization.

"**S**" stands for specific. Our goals must be specific, and it requires you to state what exactly you want to do. You must include action words.

"**M**" stands for measurable. Having the ability to evaluate and analyze progress is critical to your success. As you execute, you will gain priceless experience on what works and what doesn't work, thus driving course corrections. A former commander of mine told me early in my Air Force career; you can't change what you can't measure. Make sure you use metrics or data targets so your goal is quantifiable.

"**A**" represents achievable. Your goals need to be realistic and within your ability. You don't want to set manageable goals that don't stretch you, nor do you want to set goals that set you up for failure due to a lack of expertise or time needed to accomplish it.

"**R**" stands for relevant, ensuring it's in alignment with your business and fits into your overall life's mission and strategy. Your goals should pass the "So what?" test.

"**T**" stands for time-bound, or when you plan to get it done. You can't leave your goals open-ended. They need to be phased across a certain amount of time—whether daily, weekly, monthly, quarterly, etc. You must ensure that you make a date or time frame specific.

The power of goal setting isn't just a cliché or something that hasn't been proven. There is a wealth of scientific research on the benefits achieved from goal setting, such as its direct link to achieving success. Furthermore, research has shown that those individuals who write their goals down are 33 percent more successful than those who chose to only formulate their goals inside of their minds. The study showed that individuals who set goals and sent weekly progress reports to friends were able to accomplish significantly more than those who did not.

I have personally seen this in one of my mastermind groups, where we hold one another accountable weekly. We share weekly, intermediate, and long-term goals to measure progress and provide feedback/advice whenever a fellow member runs into challenges along the way versus them approaching it alone. The author of *Think and Grow Rich*, Napoleon Hill, defined masterminds as the coordination of knowledge and effort of two or more people who work toward a definite purpose in the spirit of harmony.

RETIREMENT EXECUTION PLAN

I relocated to a new duty station in late 2020, and one of my former non-commissioned officers who worked for me at my last unit reached out to me on Facebook to get some time on my calendar. Our conversation was a typical conversation I have with investors looking to scale their portfolios. This is one of the reasons why I decided to launch my real estate investing YouTube channel at the beginning of 2021. One of the most rewarding parts of it has been the thirty-minute strategy sessions I have to help new investors set up their strategic real estate investing plan to accelerate their journey.

We started the conversation by catching up on how the families had been doing and how busy things were back at my old unit. From there, we transitioned into his real estate plans. He wasn't new to real estate. He had two rental properties he managed in Alaska while living in Florida, where he planned to retire. One of the houses cash-flowed exceptionally well, and the other barely broke even and had a lot of capital expenditures or major systems that were nearing the end of life, such as the roof and HVAC system. He decided to sell the latter and capture his equity built up over the years to ramp up his investments in the local Panama City, Florida, market.

His question to me was, how do I get started? I responded with a question to identify what he wanted his portfolio to look like at retirement. He needed roughly $4,500 a month in passive income, and he was planning to retire in three years. Armed with that information, I knew the average rental in the Panama City market would easily cash flow around $400 a month. Using this cashflow, he will need to purchase roughly eleven houses over the next three years, which breaks down to four houses a year or one house every quarter. From there, we jumped into the execution phase of my single-family investing course. We discussed how to go about finding and buying a house once a quarter and implementing the proper strategy to get him to his three-year goal. It's just that simple. He walked away with a bulletproof plan to obtain his goal. The only remaining piece is the consistent execution to see the plan through.

Goal setting isn't a new fad or strategy that recently arose in society. Actor, comedian, and TV show host Steve Harvey gave a motivational speech after one of his shows discussing just this. The topic was how to become successful in life, and he shared an essential principle to finding success. Steve spoke to the audience in a very excited yet serious tone, "People don't have what they want because they don't have it written down! It's a vital piece to success. It's a principle of success that every wealthy person knows. I don't know anybody wealthy that doesn't have a vision board. I don't know anybody wealthy that doesn't have any stuff written on a piece of paper.

"I know a lot of people who are doing well. We have discussed at great lengths; they showed me some of their vision boards and I said, 'Wow, I need to go back and change mine.' If you do not have it written down, your chances of it happening are reduced drastically. It's a principle of success that you have to have everything you want written. It's in the Bible...

Habakkuk 2:2 says, 'Write the vision and make it plain so that he who reads it will run to it. And even though it tarry, that means it takes a long time, wait for it for surely it will come at an appointed time.' I dare you to try it... If you can think it, you can achieve it. That's not a theory...it's a habit of all successful people." I agree 100 percent. I remember when I first realized the power of writing my goals down as if it were yesterday.

GOAL SETTING FROM THE OTHER SIDE OF THE WORLD

I originally never knew the power of visualizing and writing down your goals to manifest them. I officially started to keep a journal and write down my goals during a six-month deployment to Kuwait from March to September 2018. I was doing a lot of professional enrichment—from reading multiple books to working to set up my real estate business for success once I returned home. I would write down my goals and dreams for my life, family, and my business every morning upon waking. I would write down my goal to be the best Christian husband, father, brother, son, and friend that I could be. I wanted to be the best investor home buyer in Panama City, Florida, help ten families sell a property, make $100,000 in profit, and create $10,000 in passive income in the next year. I wrote down my goals daily and became fully committed to making them happen. I wrote them down and went to work.

Being deployed in a support role provides so much time to focus on building a better you, whether physically or mentally, due to the amount of downtime in between shifts. Every morning, I would wake up, write down my goals, walk outside to the shower trailer, get dressed, and head into the office to work on my day job. I was Deputy Chief, Cyber Operations for Inherent Resolve by day and entrepreneur by night!

Although I was thousands of miles around the world, I was still in acquisition mode with mailing flyers to absentee homeowners, cold calling, and working on my website for motivated sellers. By the time I finished work, hit the gym and ate dinner, everything in the US was just getting started. I would be working in the computer lab to build out my website or make cold calls outside the recreation center while sitting at a picnic table. It wasn't uncommon for me to work up until midnight local time.

We were able to complete a couple of wholesale transactions early on while I was deployed. However, I didn't have a partner at home to facilitate my real estate transactions since my wife was pregnant and taking care of two kids. So, in the second half of my deployment, I focused on implementation once I returned home, charting out processes, new trends and crafting an overall marketing strategy for success.

Steve said during his story earlier sometimes your vision may take longer than you think. I can attest to this as I was motivated and ready to execute once I returned home to Florida. However, my plan was hastily set back less than a month upon my return home by the natural disaster caused by Hurricane Michael! We evacuated two days before the storm hit Panama City, Florida, with our third child being born five days later in Mobile, Alabama. The next six months would have our family moving from short-term rental to short-term rental from Destin, Florida, to Panama City Beach to Rosemary Beach before moving back into our remodeled home in March 2019.

It was tough with the long days and long commutes. I was director of operations for a test and evaluation unit with about seventy airmen whose families and homes had been impacted just as my family. Many who lost their homes left on humanitarian assignments since there was little to no housing inventory in the local area. Despite all the personal and logistical challenges we faced, we were able to bring our mission back online in only fifty-five days, and we were starting to normalize the rebuilding process for the base.

Initially, I thought the 159-miles-per-hour hurricane winds that shredded our local community was an enormous setback. However, it was a setup for everything I had previously been writing down in my journal that I wanted. I recall listening to Dr. Eric Thomas, ET the Hip Hop Preacher, discuss how his business was created during the 2008 financial crisis. It's uncomfortable as hell going through adversity and walking through the valleys of life. Thankfully, every challenge and situation only presents an opportunity if you have prepared yourself for the moment and have the vision to recognize it.

We had thousands of damaged homes and families in need in our community, and we were prepared to assist in rebuilding homes for families to live in but assisting in rebuilding their lives too! In 2019, we completed nine real estate transactions and made well over $100,000 in profit, helped sixteen families, added five rentals to our portfolio, and made a lasting impact in our community that continues to this day. I'm living proof that writing your goals down daily will pay off!

GOALS TO GRADUATE

I want to share with you a story of a close, dear friend of mine, Roderick Robinson. We grew up together and played high school basketball together. We were all in the same circle of friends, and after graduation, the majority either went to the University of Alabama or the other school close to the Alabama/Georgia border. Upon him departing for college and going off on his own, he didn't do so well. His transition wasn't seamless and took a detour from the traditional path. It was more of a culture shock for him. He had access to things he'd never had access to before.

If you knew where we grew up, you would know going to college was like being in a new country. He tried to make both school and his personal life work for so long, but he continuously failed to find that proper balance. After more than five years in college, his financial circumstances changed, and he was forced to work full time to pay bills and keep his head above water. This was when he hit rock bottom, and it seemed as if he wasn't going to make it.

He recounted one time during this period when he was homeless. He didn't have a place of his own. He told me, "A lot of times I slept in my car. You know I was too prideful to let anyone know I didn't have anywhere to stay! I was working at Walmart distribution center, and I was going to work at four o'clock in the evening, getting off at two o'clock in the morning, I would drive thirty minutes back toward campus, sleep, and be back in class at eight o'clock until 2:45 p.m. and off to work to do it all over again!"

And over those months and years of failures and setbacks, and never really setting any goals to hold himself accountable, he developed learned helplessness. Webster defines learned helplessness as a condition in which a person suffers from a sense of powerlessness, arising from a persistent failure to succeed. During our conversation, he exclaimed, "I felt like I couldn't make both things work. Although I hadn't succeeded, I was more mature about life in general and making better decisions, but I felt like I just could not graduate. I don't know if you know it, but it was well after all of you graduated, and I was married, and my daughter was born before I obtained my bachelor's degree from Auburn University. It did not happen until I broke the curse of helplessness and set goals for myself."

For him, it was becoming more accountable to both himself and others in his circle to give him the motivation to figure out a plan he could execute to set him up for success. Accountability is so critical to becoming self-aware of everything present in your life. Webster defines accountability as an obligation or willingness to accept responsibility for one's actions. It doesn't have to be elaborate or a formal mastermind. It can be as simple as having conversations regularly with your spouse or significant other, a group of close friends, or coworkers.

I have seen religious organizations have groups or forums set up to bring people together around certain causes to assist them in setting goals to break through the obstacles in their lives. However, regardless of how you bring it all together, the common denominator starts with you!

You can't pick and choose when and where you want to be accountable. Because at the end of the day, accountability is a critical component in the difference between success and failure. Accountability isn't a one-time thing; it's an all-the-time thing that goes hand in hand with measuring progress en route to accomplishing our goals. Those who are accountable look for solutions to challenges and setbacks and never accept failure. Today, my friend Rod continues to set the bar high and strive for success. He has established himself as a leader in logistics and operations management and currently works as high-level area manager at a top Fortune 500 company.

IMPLEMENTATION

Goal setting is a critical foundation to obtain success in real estate investing. I shared the goal-setting perspective of Michael Jordan and how he leveraged goal setting to achieve his greatness. Have you fully defined your real estate goals for the next six months, one year, five years? It's never too late to get back on track to set yourself up for long-term success. Spencer's story was truly inspirational as he laid out how he set goals to transition away from his six-figure corporate job into multifamily investing. Also, I shared the brief story of how I walked one of my former coworkers through how to set his short-term and intermediate real estate goals to generate enough passive income for retirement. Lastly, I shared the motivating story of my friend Rod and how he had to set goals to graduate from college.

At this point, it should be clear that setting goals is extremely important to reach success in life. However, don't forget those goals need to be SMART: Specific, Measurable, Achievable, Relevant, and Time-Bound. Leveraging this principle will ensure you never lose sight of your daily actions and how they integrate into your long-term goals for success. For those who haven't set their goals, I have shared a part of my goal-setting framework used by my new real estate investor mentees to help define their goals.

REAL ESTATE GOAL EXERCISE

Take a few minutes to write your short-term real estate goals that you want to accomplish in the next year. Circle your top two goals and number them in order of priority.

A. _____

B. _____

C. _____

D. _____

E. _____

Next, take a few minutes to write your long-term real estate goals that you want to accomplish in the next five to ten years. Circle your top two goals and number them in order of priority.

A. _____

B. _____

C. _____

D. _____

E. _____

REAL ESTATE ACTION PLAN

For each one of your goals, walk through the next sequence to create an executable action plan.

1. What steps do I need to take to achieve this goal?

2. How much time will it take?

3. What obstacles could get in the way of me achieving these goals?

4. What reward or value will I receive from accomplishing this goal?

CHAPTER 6

GRIT

———

*"Success is not final; failure is not fatal: It is
the courage to continue that counts."*

WINSTON CHURCHILL

MY INSPIRATION

The most compelling display of GRIT has, hands down, been
the example demonstrated by my mom, Ruth Lynum. For over
twenty years, she worked as a phlebotomist in the laboratory
at our local hospital in our quaint little town of about twelve
hundred. She worked long hours and sometimes double shifts,
spending most of the time walking from hospital room to
hospital room on her feet. She lived the example and always
pushed my sister and me to do our best and always give
maximum effort. She would always tell me, "I don't care even
if you're cleaning floors as a janitor; you be the best janitor
you can be and take pride in your work!"

After I left for college in 2000, she took a new job at a hospital located over eighty miles away from our house and a

1.5-hour commute each way. She worked the evening shift and was forced to travel the pitch-black highway swarming with deer. Over one year, she unfortunately had two head-to-head encounters as they aimlessly walked across the rural highways of Alabama at night. She would travel these roads for the next five years until she retired. Ultimately, her sacrifice paid for me to drive an almost new car while I was in college without having to work a job until my last year of school. Despite all the challenges and long days, she never complained one time and put in the work.

In December 2018, she had a severe stroke that forced her to walk with a cane and left her with no use of her right hand. Despite these physically limiting challenges, she kept pushing to remain strong and independent, not needing mercy or pity from anyone. I would speak with my parents at least once a day. She would say, "Hey, baby, how are you doing today?" I would tell her I was doing good, and I had just finished up my Air Force workday. Then she would let me know how she was feeling. If she had an accident and fell during the day, she would let me know and tell me she was all right and not to worry.

My mom passed away in June 2021 as I finished my draft manuscript for my publisher. As I stood beside her bed in ICU and in hospice for those two weeks, I intently examined the healing scars on her paralyzed right hand as well as the scars and healing scabs on her knees from the most recent of falls. It saddened me tremendously the level of pain she endured over the last few years and the feeling of helplessness on my part to prevent it. After her passing, the following months were daunting as I completed my writing and kept

Operation Invest moving along while creating a new normal. However, if I only have a tenth of the courage and grit she has shown, I know I will be able to sustain and continue to make her proud!

Life is going to happen to all of us, whether we are in the hot pursuit of our dreams or just going through life aimlessly as a boat without a rudder. So why not live on purpose and never subside to a fear of failure or stop in our tracks when faced with challenging situations. We all have doubts about our abilities and skills from time to time, but those who choose to keep moving in faith are victorious. In basketball, we say you miss every shot you don't take. I always recall the analogy for FEAR I picked up years ago from my dad's sermons. FEAR is simply, False Evidence Appearing Real. The sooner you can realize your greatness, the sooner you will be able to obtain your success not only in real estate but in every facet of your life.

In Angela Duckworth's book *Grit*, she provides the results of her years analyzing her students and the traits that led to success. She defined grit as passion and sustained persistence applied toward long-term achievement with no concern for rewards or recognition along the way. Ultimately, your passion is what it all comes down to.

Angela also shared her viewpoint on passion and its impact on accomplishing goals. She insisted passion is not about having something you care about. She exclaimed, "What I mean is that you care about that same ultimate goal in an abiding, loyal, steady way. You are not capricious. Each day, you wake up thinking of the questions you fell asleep thinking about.

You are, in a sense, pointing in the same direction, ever eager to take even the smallest step forward than to take a step to the side, toward some other destination. At the extreme, one might call your focus obsessive. Most of your actions derive their significance from their allegiance to your ultimate concern, your life philosophy. You have your priorities in order."

FRAUD, FLOOD, AND FIRE

Real estate investing isn't exempt from challenges, whether it is a problem tenant, fraudulent property management companies, floods, or an apartment unit fire. One of the most challenging real estate investments stories I have ever heard contained all the above! I ran across this investor on Jerome Myer's "Multifamily Missteps" podcast. During this episode, Randy Langenderfer shared his experience as a limited partner in a multifamily syndication located in Port Arthur, Texas, 150 miles east of Houston, Texas.

The apartment syndication was led by three general partners (GPs) who had found a 225-unit apartment built in the early 1980s owned by a developer. We will discuss more about general partners in chapter 11, which is dedicated to apartment investing. Their original plan was to leverage a bridge (short-term) loan, bring occupancy up from 77 percent to 90 percent for days, and refinance it. After only thirteen months, in September 2015, they refinanced the property and received 60 percent of their initial investment back. Things were running smoothly and right on schedule, so they thought.

In February 2016, they received news from the general partners that the property management company committed fraud by misstating occupancy and the amounts of rent received. These actions led to the mortgage company stepping in to manage all the funds for the property via lockbox. They had to find a new property manager, which had to be approved by the bank. It went on for months as the team tried to stabilize the property, understand what happened, and to complete renovations. However, in September 2017, Hurricane Harvey hit the Gulf Coast Texas area and wiped out 112 units on the first floor with three feet of floodwater penetrating.

This was almost catastrophic with the reduction of cashflow from those units required. Now, they started to fall behind on property payments. The bank slowed down on their renovation budget, which caused the lead general partner to put in between $400,000 and $500,000 of his own capital to prevent foreclosure. They continued to make progress until July 2018, when a fire broke out on the property, took out fifteen units, and subsequently killed three young children left at home alone while their mother took a sick sibling to the hospital.

Despite the fraud, a flood, a fire, and over $400,000 of personal capital, the general partner team found the grit to lead the project across the finish line in the middle of a pandemic in 2020! They continued to persevere and make all the necessary renovations to make the deal back profitable. The general partner team lead was able to sell in 2020 and give all the investors their money back with zero gain over six years, but no money lost! The GP lead could get back almost 95 percent of his capital invested in keeping the deal above water during the operation period. No one could have predicted all these events would have happened, but the team decided to persevere. At the onset of those obstacles, they could have walked away and left their investors to lose their investment, but they showed an extreme amount of integrity and grit to get the job done!

BALL BOY TO MVP

Growing up, I was extremely passionate and enjoyed both watching and playing the game of basketball. During the nineties, everyone wanted to be like Mike! Michael Jordan deified gravity and took the game to a whole new level with his athleticism and high-flying, tongue-wagging dunks. In eighth grade, I went to tryouts for basketball and made the team. I wasn't a natural talent and didn't play a whole lot. I was only five feet, seven inches in eighth grade and maybe 140 pounds, soaking wet! However, I loved the sense of brotherhood that came from being on the team and the prestige of making the cut and being on the team. I didn't have any brothers growing up, so this was the closest thing for me. We won more games than we lost, and I had a great time just being on the team and learning the game.

After getting a taste of the baller life in eighth grade, I tried out for the junior varsity team my freshmen year. It was tough. You had guys in the ninth, tenth, and eleventh grade all trying out for a handful of open spots on the team. The competition was fierce. Everything was on another level, from the drills to the pressure, to performing while being continuously assessed by the coaching staff. I came up short. I didn't make the cut. It was a gut-wrenching blow and self-esteem killer when I initially heard the news.

My friend Tommie's dad was the junior varsity (JV) coach, and he gave me the opportunity to work as the team manager for the season. I was back on the team but in a different capacity. This gave me a wonderful opportunity to see two high-performing teams operate from the practice court to bitter rival games on the road. Losing was an anomaly. Our JV team never lost more than two or three games the entire season. Our varsity team was no push-over. We had multiple Division I and II and junior college caliber athletes. I learned so much that year about the intangibles of the game and how much the little things mattered!

My sophomore year, I made the junior varsity team. I learned my weaknesses and worked on them. I practiced on my jump shot and honed my skills. I didn't start, but I was able to contribute to the team and had a lot of fun along the way. In my junior year, I became a starter, and the game began to slow down for me; I was able to start seeing plays develop on the floor and have a larger impact on the game. I became more of a scorer and motivator that year. We won the Clarke County JV tournament, and I was recognized on the All-County team.

All my hard work was paying off. Over the summer, I was putting in the work. I didn't have a basketball goal at home, so I made my way a couple of miles to my cousin's house, where he and I and a couple of other neighborhood kids would battle it out, playing one-on-one or two-on-two for hours at a time. Here on the oak tree-shaded dirt court is where I perfected my arsenal of moves on the court and my love for competition.

In my senior year, I was named starting forward on our varsity team. All my hard work had paid off. My dream was to play varsity basketball and to have an opportunity to play in front of the large, packed gymnasiums. I didn't shy away from the moment. I averaged eleven points and nine rebounds a game. We won our county tournament that year, along with our 4A Area championship. Unfortunately, we lost to the Childersburg Tigers and Gerald Wallace, who went on to play fourteen years in the NBA. The season culminated with me being named team most valuable player for our varsity team.

I now realize how great an accomplishment it was to go from being the water boy to the MVP of the team. I reflect on what would have happened if I had chosen to give up and accept temporary defeat. You know the thoughts that pop in your mind when you face challenges in life or words that come out of the mouths of others who have succumbed to personal defeat: "You will never be great. You will never make the team; stick to just getting good grades." I didn't buy into the defeated mindset and walk away from the challenge. Life is no different. We all will face challenges in life that will require us to dust ourselves off and get back up and in the race for our dreams.

In the military, grit is almost a necessity. Our mission accomplishment can mean life or death for those depending on our success. As a real estate investor, the stakes aren't as high, but they are important when we start investing both our personal money and that of our private investor partners. Effort has a much larger impact on your success than talent alone. There are always smarter and more knowledgeable people in the world; however, most don't show up consistently. Furthermore, most people don't operate within their true passion, which limits their overall effectiveness. As real estate investors, we can recall the importance of obtaining financial freedom and achieving our passive income goals to motivate us through those tough moments.

TO BE OR TO DO

In my Air Force career, my long-term goals and aspirations hit a crossroad on whether I would continue to pursue a higher rank and a job as a commander or focus on achieving financial freedom while teaching others along the way. When the moment came, it was a normal, routine workday in early spring 2021 as I was settling into my new job. I loved it. I was back in the northern Virginia area and working in another joint environment with sister service military members, civilians, and contractors. "Away from the flagpole" is how my mentor, Mr. Sherman Elliott, described being away from the core Air Force structure and my primary career field.

Anyway, I came into the office following my normal tradition of logging in to my computers and checking to see what's happened since the last shift. There wasn't anything out of the norm, so I moved along to check my Air Force email, and there it was. "You are receiving this email because we believe you are in an eligible year group for the Materiel Leader/ Command Candidate Board." I sighed as I knew this day was coming, but with how busy we had been the last three months, the thought about applying for command hadn't come to the front of my mind. I paused and just sat there staring at the screen.

I recounted in my mind my first time going through the process and being selected to meet the board on my first look. My record and experience were above average, with my last stratification placing me number two out of 154 of my field grade officer peers in my parent organization with about 2,100 members. I was slated to move the following year, so the timing was perfect. I didn't receive one job interview.

I remember asking my commander if he had spoken on my behalf with any of the potential organizations hiring, and he responded with, "No, I haven't; I've been busy." At that point, I knew it would be a long shot being selected with no one advocating on my behalf. It's not an immediate thing. It takes six months before all the replacements have been identified and approved at the highest level of the Air Force. Once the news dropped in October 2019, I wasn't shocked or surprised by the result, but it caused me to reflect on my goals.

A year earlier, in winter 2018, I was just returning from a six-month deployment away from the family with my wife being pregnant the entire time. This, by far, was the roughest pregnancy of the three for her, and I was nowhere to be found. We train all the time to be proficient at our jobs and accomplish the mission, but not a lot can prepare you for being absent from your family for an extended period. This weighed heavily on me! So, with no command job on the horizon, it was time to apply for new positions so we could relocate to our next duty station.

I listed out my top fifteen job locations, with the top five being Huntsville, Alabama, so I could lead a large joint acquisition program. I had a great interview with the hiring colonel, and they added me to the top of their candidate pool. I didn't get the job. I ended up with my number-eleven job back in northern Virginia. It wasn't a bad gig, but I was trying to stay within the south to be somewhat close to my aging parents. The more research I did on the job and the organization, the more I liked it. So much so, I declined meeting my commander board that spring so I could keep the job and not go through the whole process of trying to lobby for someone to help me get hired again. I would risk being hired and relocating to who knows where in charge of who knows what.

I snapped out of my daze and knew it was decision time. I was in a good organization, just promoted to a deputy management position after being in my job three months; we bought a great foreclosure with equity in it, we had friends in the area, the family was happy, and Johnny III was doing great in school, besides dropping the poop emoji in the class chat room one day. If I chose to, I could extend 1.5 years, find a new job in the DC area, and potentially retire here. Did I want to uproot the family another time to accomplish my goal of being a commander? It was gut-check time.

I thought back to one of the original aviation pioneers we studied throughout our professional military education curriculum, John Boyd. As a fighter pilot, he had fought in three wars and was undefeated. He was nicknamed Forty Second Boyd for his standing bet as an instructor pilot. Beginning from a position of disadvantage, he could defeat any opposing pilot in less than forty seconds. Unrivaled in the cockpit, his mind was also without rival as he was a warrior-philosopher as well. He was extremely polarizing with his never take no for an answer approach when he knew he was right and conviction in challenging the status quo.

Upon being passed over for promotion, Boyd was deeply affected! His biographer, Robert Coram, wrote, "This was a pivotal event in his career, as well as a personal epiphany. Often, when a man is young and idealistic, he believes that success will follow if he works hard and does the right thing. This was what Boyd's mother and childhood mentors had told him. But hard work and success do not always go together in the military, where success is defined by rank, and reaching a higher rank requires conforming to the military's value system. Those who do not conform will one day realize that the path of doing the right thing has diverged from the path of success, and then they must decide which path they will follow through life."

I'm no rebel or one with extremely polarizing views, as was Boyd, but I felt his pain. I had done everything within my power, led a billion-dollar development program, led intelligence, surveillance, and reconnaissance (ISR) operational teams forward, ranked extremely high amongst my peers and excelled in multiple joint operational environments, but for some reason it wasn't enough.

Boyd's final decision came down to one phrase: "To be or to do?" Robert Coram captured a quote from Boyd as he spoke to a group of his mentees. "One day, you will come to a fork in the road. And you're going to have to make a decision about which direction you want to go." He raised his hand and pointed. "If you go that way, you can be somebody. You will have to make compromises, and you will have to turn your back on your friends. But you will be a member of the club, and you will get promoted, and you will get good assignments."

Then Boyd raised his other hand and pointed another direction. "Or you can go that way, and you can do something—something for your country and for your Air Force and for yourself. If you decide you want to do something, you may not get promoted, and you may not get good assignments, and you certainly will not be a favorite of your superiors. But you won't have to compromise yourself. You will be true to your friends and to yourself. And your work might make a difference. To be somebody or to do something. In life, there is often a roll call. That's when you will have to decide. To be or to do? Which way will you go?"

I went the other way; I wanted to do for my current organization, do for my family, and do more immediately for those I could help outside of the military!

IMPLEMENTATION
Real estate investing can get gritty! As I write these words, we had a buyer rejected by their lender on day forty of our purchase contract. Life happens as it did with my mom suddenly passing in the middle of writing this book. I shared the story of how a real estate investor team overcame fraud, flood, and fire over the course of ownership of a multifamily project. What challenges have you overcome in your past where you have shown grit to persevere? The great thing for everyone when it comes to having grit is it is teachable. During a sit down with the Center for Healthy Minds, Angela Duckworth laid out a few tips to build more grit.

Her first recommendation was to develop your passion and your interest. Her second recommendation was to cultivate deliberate practice, which allows you to master a skill and improve performance. Her last suggestion was to find meaningfulness in whatever we do. This sense of purpose has a strong correlation to the individual's assessment of grit. Are there any current challenges in your real estate journey requiring you to have more grit? Our lives and careers are always demanding high-quality and high-quantity effort toward our goals. If you aren't where you want to be in your real estate journey, what steps do you need to take to get back on track? In our next chapter, we dive into the importance of networking, mentorship, and aligning ourselves with other like-minded investors.

CHAPTER 7

NETWORKING, MENTORSHIP, & MASTERMINDS

———

"If you want to be successful, find someone who has achieved the results you want and copy what they do, and you'll achieve the same results."

TONY ROBBINS

Your network leads to your net worth! Networking is one of the most important principles in achieving success in real estate or any other business endeavor. Most real estate investing transactions involve multiple specialties or experts for transactions to execute properly. Let's quickly look at the different roles or participants involved in a typical single-family home fix-and-flip project. You have an investor/buyer, a seller, a real estate agent or maybe two, a home inspector, an insurance agent, an attorney or title company, various contractors to give bids for the renovation effort, an appraiser, a lender or private investors for funding, and any partners/investors for a joint venture. As you can see, real estate is quite the team sport.

YOUR REAL ESTATE INVESTING GPS

Your job as an investor is to oversee the team and orchestrate them like a conductor commanding a symphony. Having the ability to have a strong network allows you to lower your overall risk by having the best people working to make sure you are successful. It is extremely important to network with other investors at local Real Estate Investor Association (REIA) events, meetups, seminars, masterminds, Facebook groups, etc. The saying your network is your net worth is 100 percent true. Let's jump into a great discussion I caught on the "DreamCatchers" podcast. This episode of Jerome Myer's podcast discussed the power of networking with multifamily investors and the host of the apartment investing show, "Adam Adams."

Social media is a great way to meet other investors and entrepreneurs to build your network, but it can only carry you to a certain point. "All the social media in the world is only going to go so far. Eventually, you've got to lock arms with a group of people and say we're going to do this thing together, and so for me, it's masterminds. I've learned through the mastermind that we set up for dads and multifamily is that getting the right people in the room can allow you to make a phone call and solve a problem where you could have spent months trying to figure it out on your own." Jerome went on to explain how he leveraged his mastermind group network when he was underwriting a two-hundred-unit deal that he was thinking about establishing a joint venture with another group of investors. He called one of his buddies from the group, explained the situation, and asked him what he thought he should do.

"I knew his family has about four thousand units, which is the reason why I felt comfortable calling him. The year before, he and his dad joint-ventured on a hundred-unit deal, and he's now to the point where he's got occupancy up to like 95 percent on a deal that was deeply distressed when they purchased it. Being able to make that call, get that feedback, and know they have a vested interest in you is a game-changer. It's great to be able to call on someone who can help you navigate a situation you aren't used to being in. We call it a GPS. You can sit in traffic, or you can use your GPS and navigate the traffic and get to your destination on time."

One of the great things I love about Jerome is that he doesn't keep his wealth of knowledge to himself. He goes over and beyond to share with others and add value to them. He created his mastermind group dedicated to dads investing in multifamily. His mission is to build up dads.

Often, we as men don't have an outlet to seek mentorship, and we kind of suffer silently. I'll never forget one of my buddy's texts to me; he's like, "hey, I'm dropping my daughter off at daycare, and she screams and cries her eyes out every time I drop her off. Do you have any suggestions or strategies on how this can be less painful?" I wrote him back. After we had that exchange a week later, she now waves at him, and he cries! They figured out how to make the transition. Most individuals won't pick up and read a book when they don't know what to do. However, if there's someone a little bit further along on the journey, we can ask the question. But it's not just that; we also deal with the multifamily business and how you scale it, how you brand and market it, how you go through and perform your due diligence and operations. The goal is to help build the collective body of knowledge, with an intense focus on that, being a better dad, being a better partner, and then being a better leader in your business.

MASTERMINDS

I routinely watch professional development videos on You-Tube—from industry experts to TED Talks. One specific video I recall is that of the famous author of *Think and Grow Rich*, Napoleon Hill, discussing the power of masterminds. He defined masterminds as two or more people who work in perfect harmony to attain a definited purpose. Mastermind groups allow you to use other people's education, experience, and influence in carrying out your plans in life. It gives you the ability to accomplish in one year more than you could accomplish without it in a lifetime if you depended entirely on your own efforts for success. Even more so today, entrepreneurs can easily become overwhelmed by trying to figure out how to organize their time, stay accountable, and make everything happen for their business or investments without losing their minds.

Napoleon presented his research basis, which had the collaboration of practically every successful entrepreneur the US produced during the past fifty years. "Their success was due to their knowledge and application of the mastermind principle. I also wish to call your attention to the fact that our great American way of life and our unmatchable system of free enterprise have been built upon the mastermind principle. The greatest document ever conceived by the mind of man is a perfect example of the mastermind principle in action. It is the Declaration of Independence, and the best evidence of the importance of maintaining perfect harmony in a mastermind Alliance may be found in the fact that the fifty-six men who signed the Declaration of Independence knew full well that it might turn out to be either a license of freedom for all mankind or a death warrant, which would cause each of the signers to be paid." One of the key benefits of a mastermind is that it provides a space to unpack difficult puzzles and dig into the challenges you're working through.

Napoleon wrapped up his speech by passing along words of wisdom for anyone looking to become successful by leveraging a mastermind. "Form a mastermind alliance with at least one person in your immediate family and at least one other person among those to whom you are selling your service. You will have gone a long way toward appropriating the great master key to success. There is no such thing as something for nothing. Everything, including your success, has a price that must be paid. A negative mental attitude can bring you nothing but failure. You are where you are and what you are because of your mental attitude with which you relate yourself to other people. Remember, your mental attitude is the one and only thing over which you have complete control.

Success is something that must be earned in advance. "Success is the knowledge with which to get whatever you want from life without violating the rights of others and by helping others to acquire. There is a known formula for the attainment of success. And it is as definite and certain as are the rules of mathematics or the principles of science. This thing called success is a very profound and interesting thing because the line of demarcation between success and failure is so slight that it is often hard to tell where one ends and the other begins." Tony Robbins says the quality of your life is most often a direct reflection of the expectations of your peer group. Ultimately, to reach the pinnacle of your abilities, you need to surround yourself not only with those who have been there but also those actively working on getting there.

MY FIRST MASTERMIND

I joined my first mastermind group, The WarRoom, in spring 2020. I was introduced to the group from another Air Force officer and investor, Mr. Blake Dailey at Tyndall AFB, Florida, whom I recently met. This itself is a true testament to the benefit of networking and sharing your vision and goals with other like-minded people. He had a few questions about my experience in the local real estate market. Afterward, he shared with me information about this military, veteran-centric real estate mastermind group he was a part of. At that point in time, I was extremely busy with real estate. We were in the middle of a refinance, kicking off a new fix-and-flip project and just recently completed a walk-through of the eighteen-unit apartment I was trying to negotiate the purchase price.

Up until that point, I never had a mentor to assist me in building my real estate investing business, and I was acclimated to reading and studying concepts and executing on my own. Mastermind groups can bolster a sense of connectivity and conversation, help keep your business moving forward, and they can provide critical insights for leveling up faster in your business. After learning more about multifamily and seeing the power of networking back at a multifamily seminar in October 2018, I knew I needed to find the right group to continue growing. It took me almost another month before I reached out to Dave Pere, the mastermind group founder, to join up. This single decision took my real estate portfolio and investing business to another level.

I had to wait a couple of weeks to be placed in a squad with four or five other investors based on the inflow of new members. I eventually ended up in the gold squad. We had a straightforward battle rhythm meeting every week on Sunday evenings as a group. Our plan was structured and aligned to maximize results for the squad. We kick off our meetings to capture our successes from the previous week and the highs/lows of the week.

Next, we dive into our accountability for those tasks/goals we gave ourselves to complete the following week. After everyone has had a chance to comment and provide their responses, we transition to the "Hot Seat," which is a thirty-minute focus session for one of the team members. We usually cycle everyone through unless they defer. The Hot Seat allows the member to present a challenge they are facing in their investing journey that the group can provide feedback, suggestions, and referrals to assist. My second week with the group had me on the Hot Seat, sharing my real estate journey and experience thus far and my current apartment deal that I recently got under contract.

It was mid-March, and at this point, I had the apartment under contract and was in the middle of the due diligence period. Additionally, COVID-19 was starting to become a larger threat starting to bear down on life as we knew it. After sharing the details of the deal, I had one of my gold squad members Rory Compton approach me after the following week's meeting about coming into the deal as a general partner (GP) and raising some capital. I'll talk more about the syndication construct and the role of a GP in our multifamily chapter. This was a blessing from God!

Our purchase price for the apartment was $1.05 million, and the credit union required a 20 percent down payment, $210,000, plus $13,000 in closing cost. I had a couple of private investors that were originally slated to invest, but the unexpected tanking of the stock market and businesses being forced to close their doors made it an extremely tough time to invest for some. Rory was able to step in and raise $75,000 for the deal, which allowed me to leave enough capital in my business to keep on track. From day one, based on our appraisal, we had over $200,000 in equity with a solid business plan to add $150,000 over the next year. Without joining the mastermind and Gold Squad, who knows how my first multifamily deal would have gone down!

MORE THAN JUST REAL ESTATE

Another benefit of a mastermind group is accountability. All of us are veterans, with some still on active duty, so we are fairly disciplined already. However, it's hard to get in front of your peers and tell them you fell short of reading ten pages every day, working out, calling five brokers during the week, getting new postcards sent out, or whatever the task may be. We constantly push each other to grow and never settle! We are there for one another on a personal level. Whether it's dealing with a spousal situation or losing a parent, our group has been there for one another to help rally behind each other when it's needed. Our initial bond was made through real estate, but it has grown to be a pillar foundational in our success in multiple areas of our lives. Without a doubt, being in this group has changed my real estate and life journey for the better!

I have seen apartment investors with no portfolio and no deal track record go from zero to over 200 units in less than a year. They were fortunate enough to have a seasoned mentor who introduced them to a broker they have done deals with before. As I perform consulting calls with more and more aspiring investors, I realize everyone cannot process information and execute successfully with little to no guidance along the way as I did. Mentorship allows you to shortcut the process and avoid those pitfalls others have fallen into. Wisdom is learning from others mistakes instead of your own mistakes.

During the podcast episode I mentioned earlier in the chapter between Jerome and Adam, the host Adam shared an experience from leading a mastermind group. Adam shared he was a member of a couple of mastermind groups. "I love mastermind groups as it really helps you grow who you are as a person. I run a mastermind group, but these mastermind groups are very much focused on just business. I remember a time that I got vulnerable, I jumped out, and I said something in this mastermind group we were in." They were in West Palm Beach, and Adam was really working to build his company within the multifamily syndication space. There were a lot of things happening, and he was really working to scale his company's brand in front of other people and get his podcast out while working on a couple of deals that they closed that were having some challenges.

"I remember trying to think and consider what am I going to talk about today in the mastermind. I could talk about this or this or this or this because there's a lot of challenges. When I got up in front of the room, I just came to tears, and all I said was, I just want to spend time with my kids. I am so focused on success in business, growing, and going to the next level that I'm leaving my kids behind. There were a bunch of people around. It wasn't necessarily the right place for that because it was more about business. But what was interesting is the support that I got after just being completely transparent, not trying to pretend like I was the best dad in the whole world, and I just let them know this is what I'm challenged on. I want to spend more time with my kids, but I don't know how."

Luckily, he was in good company because many people in the room had the same challenge, and they were already very successful. "You had multiple individuals in the group with thousands of apartment units and net worth's ranging from tens of millions of dollars to hundreds of millions of dollars, and they had gone through the same thing." He received guidance and insight on how to fix it, and it made a tremendous difference in his life.

IMPLEMENTATION

If you are a hard charger and self-motivated, you can probably figure out how to become successful at being a real estate investor. However, you will make mistakes along the way. Your hope is none of them are catastrophic and cause you to lose money and time. In a study by Career Horizons, research shows that 70 percent of all jobs are not published publicly on job listing sites, and up to 80 percent of jobs are filled through personal and professional networks of current employees.

Networking and mastermind groups lower your risk level while simultaneously increasing your ability to achieve success and wealth faster. At the end of the day, you want group members who will go "all in" with you: setting large goals, having determination, big dreams, and passion. Your hunger will drive your success, but you must surround yourself with other like-minded investors choosing to live their passion. This principle goes back as far as the sixth century BC. Confucius wrote, "If you are the smartest person in the room, then you are in the wrong room." If you take his advice, you can achieve all your life's dreams. You become like those you hang around.

Additionally, I challenge you to find at least one multi-day real estate event to attend in the next six months. Back in October 2021, I attended my first in-person real estate investing event for the entire year, Flip Hacking Live, led by Bill Allen, and to say it was phenomenal is almost an understatement. I met dozens of real estate investors and heard great presentations with tactics I can use in my business.

Do you have a real estate mentor assisting you on your journey? Have you ever considered joining a mastermind? If you want to become a successful real estate investor, then you must start hanging around more successful real estate investors.

I encourage you to perform some research and decide if a results-focused mastermind is right for you. In 2021 alone, I have spent over $40,000 to join two mastermind groups to broaden my network and to help take my real estate business profit from six figures to seven figures! If you are interested in learning more about my *Millionaire Real Estate Success Mastermind*, then simply go to www.JohnnyLynum.com. From there, you can sign-up for one-on-one consultation.

This is the last chapter in this section dedicated to the habits and traits of successful real estate investors. The next section will dive into those real estate investment strategies you can implement immediately to build your million-dollar portfolio. Never forget, you are the average of the four or five people in your life you spend the most time around!

CHAPTER 8

FINANCING REAL ESTATE DEALS

———

*"Rich people use debt to leverage investments
and grow cash flows. Poor people use debt to
buy things that make rich people richer."*

GRANT CARDONE

If you listen and follow Dave Ramsey, you probably break out in cold sweats when you hear the word debt. There is no lack of negative perceptions when it comes to talking about debt today. On the surface, he is right when he insists everyone should avoid bad debt or consumer debt like the plague. However, this is not the case for savvy real estate investors who use good debt to buy cash-flowing appreciating assets. Good debt allows you to build long-term wealth by leveraging debt instead of paying 100 percent cash-to-purchase assets.

There are a myriad of financing options when it comes to purchasing real estate. You have traditional lending for primary residences, commercial loans, seller financing, home equity lines of credit (HELOC), lines of credit (LOC), credit cards, hard money loans, private investor loans, Individual Retirement Accounts (IRAs), and of course, cash.

CREATIVE FINANCING

I recall one of my most memorable creative real estate financing deals to date. It was 2018, and we were displaced after Hurricane Michael devastated the Panama City area. I subsequently shifted my marketing three hours away to Mobile, Alabama, where my parents were living. I pulled an absentee owner list and started a postcard campaign looking for value-added properties to purchase. After only one month of marketing, I had a warm lead with an investor/builder owner interested in having someone take over his monthly payments and management of the property since he was tired of being a landlord. The house was a 1,400-square-foot starter home built in 2006 close to downtown with a $39,000 mortgage balance, $380 mortgage payment, and $72,000 appraised value. I was able to craft a win-win solution by taking over the payments and management. I established a land trust to take ownership to avoid activating a due on sale clause with the mortgage company. In the end, I paid a whopping $1,453.69 (closing cost) to take over ownership with the existing loan still in place.

I have used every loan I listed above in my ten-plus year investing journey. To be successful in real estate, financing creativity is a must. Starting with limited capital, I leveraged debt to buy my first rental property. Upon purchasing my first flip in 2015 in Alexandria, Virginia, I leveraged a hard money loan, personal capital for my down payment, and my line of credit and credit cards for the renovation cost. Unfortunately, I didn't have a mentor/coach, a network of other investors in a mastermind, nor did I have experience leading a fix-and-flip project yet to obtain better terms.

A hard money lender is a nontraditional lender that lends money based on the property used as collateral. Most times, the capital comes from either an individual, a private equity fund, or other group of investors. I met with multiple companies shopping my deal around before finding a local hard money lender who would lend to me. He wasn't cheap, and I cringe when I look back at the terms he charged me compared to better rates/terms and the large amount of lenders available today. He gave me a six-month term for $230,000, including a $40,000 renovation draw with a whopping $23,000 loan discount added at loan payoff.

If I had to do it all over again, I would still do it because we learned so much from that project that we still take with us in every project we execute. Luckily, the lending landscape is a lot better now, and there are more opportunities to partner on deals to get started.

After signing the term sheet for the loan product, it was a huge relief despite the terms, but the due diligence work began. Leading up to receiving the term sheet, I had to provide my financial statement and a list of recent projects, a schedule of real estate owned, and our estimated renovation budget. This hard money lender wasn't a large lender and was essentially a single individual with a high net worth. I met him at the property for his inspection, which is typical since the property secures the loan. The inspection went without a problem, and we were cleared to move forward with closing as we waited for the title work to be completed. Today, I work with a lender who started paying an individual inspector to take pictures and write a report before approving, but now they are comfortable with me just supplying pictures of the project for approval. They also perform desktop appraisals versus having a physical appraisal to assess the after-repair value.

Now, let's talk about the capital required through the process and how renovation funds were released. Initially, once we went under contract, we wired $4,300 into the escrow account for closing. After shopping around for a loan and deciding to move forward with our lender, I had to pay a $1,000 loan commitment fee up front before closing. Most hard money lenders also charge origination points or fees based on the amount of the loan. My lender waived this fee. Most hard money lenders provide the option to pay for renovation costs and hold the money in an escrow account post-closing. My lender held back $40,000, which could be accessed in two draws of $20,000 as renovations progressed along with a $250 draw fee for each draw. We had thirty days to close, which is somewhat standard, but depending on your real estate market, you may have to shorten your time to close to have a competitive offer when you are in a multiple offer situation. Lastly, at closing, we had to bring another $34,109, which represented the closing cost plus a 13 percent down payment.

We moved on from our initial hard money experience and developed more relationships with larger, more established lenders. Your lender is an intricate part of your real estate team and provides you with the means to scale your investment portfolio or fix-and-flip business faster than only using your capital. Real estate is one of the few assets where you can purchase an asset with 80 percent leverage and receive tax depreciation on an asset that appreciates while it creates cash flow. Furthermore, the bank or lender doesn't participate in the upside appreciation of the asset, and you as the owner capture 100 percent of the asset's increase in value.

PRIVATE NOTES

A perfect example of leveraging multiple funding options as an investor is my friend, Mr. Justin Melendez. I met Justin in one of my mastermind groups, and he is an active investor in the Fayetteville, North Carolina, and Augusta, Georgia, markets. Justin shared how he funded one of the most recent flip projects he picked up from a local wholesaler. After walking the property, he went out to his car to contact the wholesaler. "I sat in the parking lot, and I texted him. I said, 'Hey, I want it,' and we locked it up right there. He sent me the contract within a few minutes, and we locked it up. I recognized an opportunity, so I acted fast, but I didn't have all the money.

"There were a few reasons we didn't have the money. I had a $25,000 note that I lent to another friend who was doing a flip. It hadn't matured yet, but we were expecting it to mature within the next few weeks. With interest, it would be $27,000 when it came back. I had about $40,000 to my name and in another transaction we were selling one of our rentals, which was about another $22,000, closing a week before we would close on this new deal. But I wasn't comfortable with that, and I wanted to make sure we had the money as soon as possible so we could close on this and seize the opportunity. I reached out to my family, and luckily my brother was willing to partner with me, and he lent me $25,000, and my mom lent me $7,000."

Justin provided two different investment options based on the amount of capital invested. If you invested $10,000 or less, the investor would receive a flat 10 percent return for 180 days, which is a great return. For $10,000 and above, investors can choose a 10 percent flat return or become an equity partner and possibly receive a larger return. His brother opted for the equity position and was given a 75 percent/25 percent split. His mom invested $7,000 and received a flat 10 percent return. There were no interest payments throughout the term and no origination points. Once the project was completed, investors received their principal plus interest.

For my business, Operation Invest LLC, I primarily provide a 10 percent annualized return with a six-month term since most of our projects take around four or five months to sell or refinance. My investors access our third-party secured investor portal website to see all our offerings and to digitally sign all the documentation. All funds are wired or sent via ACH to fund a deal and when we pay out the principal and interest upon sale or refinance of the project. At the end of the year, investor tax documents can be downloaded from their account.

Another great loan for investors is commercial loans. They are usually less restrictive than traditional mortgage loans as they allow for higher loan balances with no primary residence requirement. Additionally, there isn't any federally imposed limit on the number of active loans you can have. Since these loans are given to corporate entities, the loans never show up on your credit report. However, it's not all roses and unicorns. Most commercial loans require investors to have a higher credit score than traditional mortgages. Also, commercial loans require a 20 to 30 percent down payment with shorter terms and slightly higher interest rates.

LOCAL LENDER PARTNERSHIP

As we grew our rental portfolio in Panama City, Florida, one of our local credit unions became an intricate partner on our team. As we scaled up our investing business and began to work on simultaneous projects, capital became a premium. We started sharing more of our investing journey on social media to share with others what was possible through real estate. In return, we had a couple of family members approach us about investing with us on deals. We were able to work out great terms that were mutually beneficial. However, as we moved into buying houses, all cash and paying for renovations across three houses, we leveraged our credit lines to keep operations moving forward. Once I pivoted, keeping more homes as rentals, we ran into an issue with qualifying for a loan. This was due to my credit score reflecting a high debt to income ratio because of the credit line utilization.

Through networking, I found a local lender that offered a commercial portfolio loan and could offer me a cash-out refinance for my three projects and the "subject-to" property I picked up in Mobile, Alabama. We started the loan process in November 2019 by completing an application and sending over our rental leases for each property along with the scope of work for the renovations completed on each property.

The terms weren't that great with an interest rate of 8.375 percent, 5/1 Adjustable-Rate Mortgage (ARM), 65 percent loan to value (LTV), thirty-year amortization, and a three-year pre-payment term. Next, we had appraisals ordered for each property with each one's value coming back right at our estimated valuations.

As we completed the renovation on our duplex and received tenants for both sides, we were coming into mid-December. The process dragged on for another eight weeks with underwriter request after underwriter request for additional information. During the same time, I found our apartment complex and was working the deal through a local credit union to see their terms offered.

While discussing the apartment deal, I mentioned needing to refinance a group of single-family rentals soon. Since it was out of state, he couldn't refinance my Mobile, Alabama, property, but he ran a loan estimate based on my recent appraisals. He offered me a 4 percent interest rate, 5/1 ARM, 80 percent loan to value (LTV), twenty-five-year amortization, fifteen-year term. Even with the 3 percent prepayment penalty, it was worthwhile to refinance as soon as possible. We closed with the first lender, paid off our credit lines, waited two weeks for my credit score to update, and then began the refinance process with the credit union. We refinanced the loan before we made our first payment and secured a great partnership that continues today.

Our apartment financing terms were similar, 4 percent, 80 percent LTV, 5/1 ARM, twenty-five-year amortization, fifteen-year term. Going through our portfolio refinance, I learned a ton about how credit unions work. They keep all their loans in house as they don't package them up and sell them. The loan approvals are done by a board after the business development lead presents your loan package, which comprises your credit profile, schedule of real estate-owned, and personal financial statement.

When it came to the apartment, I completed my underwriting as I analyzed the property to determine my offer price. I shared my analysis with the business loan representative, and he gave me a piece of feedback that stuck with me. He told me that when he has investors come in looking for a new loan and provide their spreadsheets and internal underwriting assumptions, it gives him confidence in their overall capability to manage and execute the business plan for the property.

We went under contract on our apartment on March 8, 2020, a couple of weeks before the country would shut down due to COVID-19, which placed an enormous amount of stress on me to get the deal closed. As I listened to other investors and podcasts, it was apparent the lending environment was starting to shift as the stock market began to tank and the economy began to come to a screeching halt! It took us 3.5 months to close, primarily due to us requiring the seller to repair a leaking water main before closing. Furthermore, the delay allowed us the opportunity to go from bringing all the required $210,000 for the 20 percent down payment to executing our first syndication.

I first learned of the syndication model back in October 2019 at my first multifamily investor conference in Orlando, Florida. One of the speakers was a syndication attorney who had recently written a book that I purchased about the topic. Previously, I created promissory notes with a fixed-rate return for some of our single-family projects where we had private investors. I took this same approach to raise private investor capital to bring to the apartment deal. As we moved into April and May, finding investors still looking to invest with all the uncertainty going on became a challenge, but I refused to give up.

I received a great referral for a syndication attorney from a couple of investors in my newly joined mastermind group. A syndication attorney specializes in Securities Exchange Commissions (SEC) law and creates the necessary documents required to comply with SEC laws. These include the private placement memorandum (PPM), subscription agreement (SA), and the operating agreement for the new entity that will take the title of the apartment. As I mentioned back in chapter 5, I brought on an additional general partner (GP), Rory Compton, whom I met a couple of months earlier in my mastermind group. He helped raise $75,000 to go with an additional $20,000 I raised from a friend. We provided our investor partners a 7 percent cash-on-cash (CoC) return, paid quarterly, two-year term, with a $20,000 equity share at the refinance milestone, which gave them a 17 percent IRR for the two years. We eventually completed the water main work and closed the deal in June 2020 in the middle of a pandemic.

RICH DAD ADVICE

One of the most well-known real estate investors and authors in the world is Robert Kiyosaki, author of *Rich Dad Poor Dad*. I recently listened to a "Biggerpockets" podcast episode he guest-appeared on to discuss real estate investing. The first property he ever purchased cash flowed twenty-five dollars each month. Today he owns 6,500 homes, and every one of them puts money in his pocket each month, and it all comes from debt! He shared his perspective on how a business's primary purpose should be to acquire real estate for you to acquire massive amounts of debt, so you can legally avoid paying taxes. His rich dad told him that to be rich, he needed to understand real estate and entrepreneurship.

His approach of leveraging debt allows him the opportunity not to pay any taxes. His approach came from Tom Wheelwright, who says taxes are used to incentivize capitalists to use debt. Real estate is so critical to America and capitalism because investors provide housing to millions of Americans. They don't teach real estate investing and financial literacy because the government needs uninformed people to pay taxes at the end of the day.

The host, Brandon Turner, shared how he leverages real estate financing to buy properties to hand down to his kids. His strategy entails buying a property when each of his kids is young and placing a fifteen-year mortgage on the houses, so the asset is paid off by the time they are ready to go off to college. He reaps the tax benefits, the cashflow over the time frame, the tenant pays off the mortgage, and his kids can use the property to pay for college or start a business after graduating high school.

One of the key themes Robert spoke about directly impacts mortgage interest rates, which is inflation. Leveraging debt to purchase real estate serves as a great hedge to inflation.

One great metric to track inflation is the consumer price index (CPI), the weighted average of the price of goods and services over time. In June 2021, the CPI jumped 5 percent for the twelve months ending in May 2021. This represented the largest annual increase since August 2008. As inflation rises, so does the cost of everyday household items we use daily as well as the price of real estate.

When interest rates are low, real estate becomes a great hedge against inflation due to the increased value and payments over time with dollars that have less buying power! Unfortunately, every time the Federal Reserve prints money, they screw over working-class people, who lose buying power because of inflation. Fortunately for investors, the price of real estate increases with inflation and the price of rent. As your rents increase, your cashflow will increase, which provides additional capital to use at your discretion to invest or pay down your principal sooner.

To take advantage of the low-interest rate and high inflation environment, Robert discussed refinancing his properties and pulling out millions of dollars to buy more assets. At that moment, he was obtaining rates at less than 2 percent, which had minimal impact on his overall cashflow from his portfolio. In the first quarter of 2021, investors bought one of every seven US homes purchased; this represented a considerable increase based on the previous three quarters when the metric was only one out of every ten homes. Additionally, Lennar Homes—one of the largest homebuilders in the United States—announced early in 2021 that it was purchasing over four billion dollars of new single-family homes and townhomes in high-growth areas to rent them.

This clearly highlights the approach of investors hedging against inflation while loan rates are low.

SELF-DIRECTED RETIREMENT ACCOUNTS

Another great way to finance real estate deals is by leveraging self-directed retirement accounts (SDRA). Whether leveraging your account or those of other investors, SDRAs give you the ability to diversify a portfolio and secure above-average returns. Author James Misko calls SDRAs the best-kept secret in real estate. You don't have to only invest in the stock market and cash deposits (CDs). Self-directed IRAs allow you to invest your own money into assets you are knowledgeable about. The largest concentration of investable cash for Americans is their retirement account. A person with investment capital is more likely to have more money in their retirement account than their personal savings account.

A self-directed retirement plan can lend money to another investor with a deal and that investor pays back the IRA or 401k plan under the promissory note terms. The retirement account is the lender on the promissory note, and the other investor is the borrower. The promissory note can be structured with monthly payments or a lump sum at the end of the agreed term. Additionally, your retirement account can receive points and interest from the lender.

Your SDRA can buy real estate too. After identifying a property for purchase, the contract to purchase the property is in the name of the SDRA and not you as the SDRA owner. Once you close on the property and start to collect rent, the expenses for the property are paid by SDRA while income from property such as rent or appreciation from the future sale goes directly to SDRA. These are just a couple of the numerous SDRA strategies that allow you to control your investment capital better.

I have current investors who partner with us on deals who leverage their self-directed IRAs to passively invest in our deals. They sign up on our investor portal and create an investment account for their SDRA. When they see an offering they would like to invest in, they simply sign the promissory note electronically as the manager of the SDRA and wire the money from the SDRA checking account. Once the project is complete, we wire the principal and interest back to the SDRA's checking account. If you have an old 401k or IRA from a previous employer, I encourage you to find more information about rolling it over into your SDRA. I am not a CPA or attorney, so please seek professional advice to assess the best strategy for your situation.

IMPLEMENTATION

Hopefully, after reading these stories and examples, you have some new ideas on leveraging debt to take your investing to the next level. As a real estate investor, one skill we didn't discuss in detail was the process of how to raise private money and the proper way to do it. Ultimately, as you grow as an investor and become more experienced, your ability to receive financing and raise private capital will increase. There is no more humbling feeling than to have someone give you their hard-earned money to invest in your ability to execute a real estate project!

When it comes to traditional financing, your credit score is extremely important along with your debt-to-income ratio.

What's your current credit score and debt to income ratio? Do you have a good relationship with a local bank or credit union? If not, I encourage you to go and sit down with one of their business development representatives and learn more about their commercial products. This will be an invaluable relationship to assist you in building a rental portfolio and long-term generational wealth. I spoke briefly about the power of leveraging a self-directed IRA to grow your retirement accounts outside the roller coaster ride of the stock market. In the next chapter, we will dive into single-family home investing.

CHAPTER 9

SINGLE-FAMILY HOME INVESTING

"Landlords grow rich in their sleep without working, risking, or economising."

JOHN STUART MILL

One of the easiest ways to get started in real estate is by investing in single-family homes. There are multiple strategies that you can use to grow your wealth. You can purchase a single-family residence, live in it for as little as a year, and transition it to a rental property. When purchasing a property as a primary residence, you have access to many different programs that require as little down payment as 3.5 percent. If you're a veteran, you can leverage your VA Loan benefit, which allows you to purchase a home with 100 percent financing or zero money down. One fact that many don't know is that you can purchase up to a four-unit building with a residential loan, including the VA loan. Overall, the single-family rental market has historically been dominated by mom-and-pop landlords who own a couple of properties and use them to fund their retirement.

Another strategy is house hacking, where you rent out individual rooms or a basement to help cover your monthly expenses. For those who can put a 20 to 25 percent down payment, you can look to purchase a rental property out of the gate for investment purposes. Some investors choose to purchase "turnkey" properties, which are simply rental properties that have been usually completely remodeled recently and have a tenant and property management already in place. This strategy allows investors a straightforward opportunity to purchase out of state in the best rental markets for future rent growth and appreciation. Next, I want to share the story of real estate entrepreneur, military wife, and mother Shannon Kiefhaber and how her family leveraged single-family investing to accomplish their investing goals.

VA LOAN TO PRIVATE LENDING

During our discussion, Shannon shared how she and her husband got started in real estate and some of the challenges they faced with their first property. She grew up in a real-estate-minded household, so she didn't have the fear that stops so many from acting, but her husband, on the other hand, did. Becoming an accidental landlord out of the gate didn't help at all. She shared, "We had a bad experience with us being in the military and having to move often. We bought our first house in Virginia Beach, and then we had to move out to California. We became first-time accidental landlords, and it didn't go well!" She continued her story, "We ended up having to evict our tenant in Virginia from across the country. My husband was like, 'That's it. I'm done. I hate real estate. It's horrible. I'm not doing it.' Some time passed, and he went off to weapon school."

Not too long after her husband left for weapon school, she found a foreclosure. She passionately continued telling her story: "I knew the area, so I had my dad go by and look at it for me, and we ended up buying it at the auction. I had to call my husband and tell him while he was in Top Gun training that I accidentally won this house!" She was really concerned, nervous, and scared. However, she didn't let the fear consume her. She said to her husband, "Listen, we had one bad experience; we're not going to let that deter us from what I know we should be doing." They were able to go through with the sale and continue building their portfolio from thousands of miles away.

Sharon went on to tell me that it wasn't always a walk in the park as they moved along their investing journey. Like all couples, they had their challenges too. In one case she could recall, they had a come-to-Jesus moment. "I felt like with being a mom, having a full-time career and then with a Navy husband, it was a lot to manage. He would return home and feel like he didn't know anything about what was going on." She sat him down and once a quarter to do a net worth analysis and review profit and loss statements. It helped calm his nerves and let her keep investing, but over time they slowly started to transition to make it a little bit more of a team effort.

"He couldn't really take over all the property responsibilities," she exclaimed. "We talked about it, and we started dividing responsibilities. He started cooking all the dinners, doing the meal planning, going to the grocery store, and helping out in that way because he liked to cook more than I did. I think it's important you know to share in the load, whatever that load is, stuff has to get done and it's all equally important."

As we concluded, I asked Shannon if she could go back in time and give herself one piece of advice, what would it be? She responded, "I would say buy a house and move every year before you have kids. We used a VA loan and purchased our first house. I wish we had bought a duplex and lived on one side and rented the other for a year, and once we lived there for a year and then moved on and repeated the process. We could have done that five times before we had kids. Being military, that was our competitive advantage, and we didn't exploit it. It always sticks with me as I wish I had exploited my competitive advantage a little more initially."

SINGLE-FAMILY INVESTING

I mentioned it in one of the earlier chapters, but I will go a little deeper into what I mean when I say you make money in real estate, not when you sell but when you buy. If you don't buy at the right price, it will be hard to make money. The caveat to that statement is if you wait and hold the property long enough, time erases most mistakes. If you overpaid, but it's still cash flowing, you would continue to pay down the principal over time and reduce your mortgage balance, and at the same time, the market continues to appreciate. Therefore, cashflow is so important. If the market value tanks 20 percent to 30 percent, all you will need to do is hold firm, continue to collect rent, and wait. I know a few investors who bought in 2007 at the top of the market, rode out a correction, paid down their principal over the last ten-plus years, and now have a sizable amount of equity in the property. Now, they have the option to sell and roll the capital into another property or invest in a large deal via a partnership or syndication.

As with anything in life, there are both pros and cons when it comes to investing in single-family homes. The barrier to entry is a lot less when compared to commercial real estate. You can buy a home for less than $100,000 versus buying a million-dollar apartment building. It's easier to perform your inspections and due diligence versus an apartment building. Furthermore, when buying an apartment, buyers usually leverage partnerships or a multiple LLC structure. This allows investors to limit their overall liability while properly structuring a company to manage the asset.

Another great advantage of the single-family asset class is that the single-family resale market is larger than the commercial market and has a larger pool of properties to choose from. On the downside, apartments provide more cashflow with less dependency on a single tenant. Additionally, apartments provide an economy of scale by having all the units in the same geographical area, usually with multiple units under the same roof.

My number-one strategy that I love the most is the buy, renovate, rent, refinance, and repeat (BRRRR) strategy. This strategy is based on purchasing a single-family home that requires some remodeling to become rent ready. I use the 70 to 75 percent rule to evaluate my deals. The purchase price plus the renovation cost estimate should equal 70 to 75 percent of the after-repair value (ARV).

Example: We have a three-bedroom, two-bathroom 1,600-square-foot home that a landlord in your neighborhood said he wanted to sell as is. Homes that size have been selling at $150 per square foot. Our contractor says it needs $35,000 in repairs. What's our max offer price?

$$ARV = 1,600 \times \$150 = \$240,000$$

$$\$240,000 \times .70 = \$168,000 - \$35,000 = \$133,000 \text{ (max offer price)}$$

Once the repairs are made and the property is rented, you should begin the refinance process while you are finishing the repairs. I love to use my local credit union as they offer great commercial loan products for local-based businesses. I own all my BRRRR properties in an LLC. It's not mandatory to use an LLC to purchase a rental property, but as you grow your portfolio, it's worth considering for liability reasons, and it allows you to take on debt in the name of the business instead of your name. Lastly, once you refinance, repeat the process. This is a perfect strategy to leverage hard money lenders, as we discussed back in chapter 8, since you are adding substantial value to the property in a short amount of time. The BRRRR method can produce great passive income and scale your real estate portfolio in a short amount of time. To make sure you have a firm grasp of the BRRRR strategy, I will share one of my personal BRRRR projects purchased in early 2021.

BRRRR

This was a unique property from the day due to how long it took to purchase it from the seller. We originally contacted the owner back in February 2020 concerning a vacant duplex they owned. They were in the middle of a dispute with their insurance company and tied up in litigation. I consistently followed up with them every six to eight weeks to check in for updates for the next six months. In October 2020, they were finally getting close to having everything resolved when the husband, whom I had never spoken with, signed a contract to sell the duplex to another person. *All that follow up for nothing*, I immediately thought, as she gave me a sincere apology for the late change of plans. However, she asked me if I would be interested in an occupied rental property they no longer wanted in their portfolio. I replied, "Of course!" grinning from ear to ear!

This property was purchased for $84,000 after a straightforward negotiation. My contractor was able to walk the property and put our renovation budget together. We planned for a $28,000 renovation budget and a thirty-to-forty-five-day construction period. I expected it to rent monthly for about $1,300 since it was in a good school district. Our hard money appraisal came back with an estimate of $158,000. One of the important clauses in our contract was that the property had to be vacant at closing. The owner had given the resident a heads up, so we weren't planning on it taking too long. However, he came down with COVID, which forced him into quarantine and delayed us three weeks.

This was a typical renovation project for us as our niche is buying homes that require cosmetic renovations with a new roof here or there. We don't knock down walls and open rooms, and we focus on homes at the median purchase price in our market or less. We primarily work with the 1960s or later homes under 2,000 square feet and with concrete slab foundations. These factors all roll up together to reduce our overall risk of surprises and unexpected issues. When we first started out renovating virtually, we paid for home inspections to identify all the issues with a property, so we would know what needed repairing outside of the obvious cosmetic items. You may consider this as well if you're just starting out and don't have a general contractor you can depend on just yet. The renovations finished around the forty-five-day mark.

We went with a new property management (PM) company for this home to diversify our management, so all our assets aren't with one management company. The PM returned with a recommended rent of $1,500, which was $200 more than expected. We received multiple applications and had a lease in less than a week! Going with a new PM company allowed us an opportunity to build another relationship with another local power broker in our market. Guess who a landlord usually notifies when they are getting ready to sell a rental? You guessed right—their property manager. Guess who the property manager calls when they get word of an off-market property someone wants to sell? Hopefully, you or me. Relationships are critical. What if a landlord is selling his portfolio of five, ten, or twenty properties? One deal can change your net worth overnight!

We leveraged our local credit union for our refinance who has a great loan product for rental properties. We secured a 75 percent loan to value (LTV), 4 percent interest rate for fifteen years, twenty-five-year amortization, with the rate adjusting every five years to the prime rate plus 3/4 points. Our bank appraisal came back at $155,000, our loan was approved for

$120,000, and our mortgage, interest, and insurance payment was set at $840 a month. Our PM cost is 10 percent of rent or $150 a month, which places our total monthly cashflow at $510 a month. Our total closing cost for both the original and refinance loan was about $5,500, and we had $1,100 in interest payments during our hold period, which put us all in $122,000 into our deal. At $155,000 value, this leaves us with $35,000 in equity. After refinancing and paying off our hard money loan and carrying cost, it leaves us with $2,000 left in the deal. Now, let's calculate our annual cash on cash return.

$2,000 / (12 * $510) = 3.06 or 306% cash on cash return each year

Now, it's time to repeat and find the next deal. Finding deals needing repairs allow you to force appreciation and start with a 20 percent or 25 percent equity position from day one.

LONG DISTANCE INVESTING

I have spoken with many aspiring investors who have lived in expensive markets such as San Diego, Washington, DC, and New York City. They shared how hard they struggled to get started in real estate investing as a direct result of a high-priced market. However, now more than any other time in history, investors can invest remotely, over long distances. After completing our first fix-and-flip project in Alexandria, Virginia, about twenty miles away from our home, we decided to transition our business ten hours away to the Birmingham, Alabama, market. It was a great learning experience as we bought and sold homes in multiple states over the next two years. After relocating back to the Washington, DC metro area in November 2020, we resumed long distance investing with buying, selling, and holding property fourteen hours away in the Panama City, Florida, market. Next, I want to share a more passive real estate investing strategy that allows you to invest in the best markets with little to no effort.

This passive investing strategy is called turnkey. This strategy is simply buying recently remodeled single-family homes with a paying tenant in place along with recommended lenders and property management companies to streamline the whole process from beginning to end. My friend Doug Spence first got into turnkey rental properties after listening to a "Biggerpockets" money podcast with Stu Grazier back in August 2018. Stu shared how he and his partner David had a bad experience with a turnkey property in Birmingham, Alabama, and how they were screwed over after purchasing a subpar property from a local turnkey provider. Ultimately, this inspired them to start their own company to provide cash-flowing real estate to active-duty military and veterans.

Doug went on to share how it all came together for him. "Around the same time that I heard Stu's podcast episode, I was reading *Long Distance Real Estate* by David Greene, and it gave me a lightbulb moment. I don't have to invest where I live! So, those two really inspired me, and I reached out to Stu and scheduled a call with him to chat about real estate."

He wasn't initially planning to buy anything from them, so they just talked about real estate and the future of Stu's new company. Ultimately, Doug decided to work with them, and he became one of the first people to buy one of their first turnkey properties in December 2018. "I liked it because it was not as daunting a task compared to putting your team together like doing a flip, especially out of state. Even if I was doing that where I was living at the time, I wouldn't have known how to do any of that stuff. I didn't know what I know now about putting a team together. I saw buying turnkey properties as a way to get my foot in the door. I've always been a strong saver and pretty frugal, which allowed me to have the capital saved up for the 20 percent down payment on a $100,000 property with cash flow from day one!"

Early in the process, they referred him to a local lender to get pre-approved for a conventional mortgage and a local property management company. "I just went with their people, and it was an overall positive experience. It was pretty easy, to be honest, and what I really liked was whenever I had questions, Stu was very responsive. He always got back to me very quickly and always had a good, honest answer. He was knowledgeable about the whole process, so that helped too. I closed on the first one in December 2018, and three months later, another property became available. I said, 'Sure, why not, since I had the cash.'" He closed in April of 2019 and got back on the waiting list.

The following month after Doug closed on his first turnkey property, he started telling friends about his great experience and the monthly cashflow he was making. Many people asked him who he knew or if he was from Milwaukee or planning to retire there. He explained how he invested there because of the economic trends and future growth expectations for the area. This concept was foreign to a lot of people, but it made great sense when leveraging the team of local experts, which is the top benefit of buying turnkey real estate. After he closed on the second property, he jumped back on the waitlist for another one. However, he didn't close on the third one until over a year and a half later, due to the number of investors ahead of him! One of the unfortunate challenges with turnkey is the length of time it takes to purchase the properties due to the extremely long waitlist. Once the word is out on the street of a great turnkey provider, their waitlist usually becomes lengthy in a short amount of time.

So, I know you are asking yourself, *How do I find someone on the other side of the United States whom I can trust to sell me a quality house that I may never even visit in person?* This was one of the questions I asked Doug during our conversation. For him, it's not about the deal but about the people. "If you're dealing with someone who's dishonest or just trying to make a quick buck, it's not going to go well." I have personally heard horror stories of investors buying properties that had lots of hidden or unaddressed issues. Sometimes, operators may try to cut corners with rehabbing the property since rehab expenses are the largest share of the overall expense for the project. "It's important to know that the deal makes sense on paper, but the most important piece is vetting the operator. You need to know why they're selling the house as a turnkey property, what their goals are, and who they've worked with in the past, obtaining referrals and talking to people that have bought from the turnkey provider. So if you are considering investing with a turnkey company, you must vet the owners."

Doug went on to share more about his turnkey experience. "What I like about Stu and David's company, Storehouse 310 Ventures, is that they're very brutally honest about everything. There were concerns that I had about one of the properties; I can't even remember which one, but the furnace was older, and their inspector told them it was an older furnace, but they last like a long time. I was not sure about the furnace, and they added a document to the contract stating if there were any issues related to that furnace for three years, they would cover any expenses related to it." Additionally, for Doug, it helped knowing they were also military as he is. "If you spend seventeen or eighteen years active duty in the military, you're not going to get that far if you're a dirtbag and you're not trustworthy. I still contacted references for them and talked to people they worked with in the past. From the very beginning of the first conversation I had with Stu, I felt this was someone that I could trust."

LONG, LONG DISTANCE INVESTING

I just shared with you how to invest long distance from anywhere in the United States. Now, I want to share a story of how an investor started investing from over four thousand miles away while living in Europe.

I first met Billy Keels in the spring of 2021 at the Mid-Atlantic Multifamily Conference where he introduced himself and shared his story. He currently resides in Barcelona, Spain, where he has lived for the last fifteen years, but he is originally from Columbus, Ohio. He started out his professional career like so many others. He began working for a couple of years and putting money away in his 401k retirement account. Life was good.

Everything was going just fine up until the 2000 dot com bubble burst! He was greatly impacted. He became distraught as his financial advisor told him not to worry since this was part of what happens and to stay calm. He continued to work and work and then this thing in 2008 happened again. This go around, he lost 33 percent of his portfolio he entrusted to Wall Street.

Just like Billy, most Americans have taken their retirement into their own hands! However, most are limited by their preferred investment vehicles, the IRA and 401(k), because they are only able to invest in the stock market. Most of us are old enough to remember the financial meltdown of 2008 that shocked Billy's financial journey and the decrease in the value of everyone's investment accounts. Unfortunately, those at retirement age felt the pain the worst. Those near retirement were forced to delay retiring and work another four to ten years in order to recapture their lost wealth.

For Billy, he emphasized Wall Street didn't take his money from him, but that he made a conscious decision to do that. However, one of the things his parents taught him was if it happens once, shame on them; if it happens twice, shame on me. At that moment, he decided it was time for him to do something completely different because he had done every-thing he was supposed to do in his financial life, but it was not working. Luckily, in 2012, he picked up *Rich Dad Poor Dad* for the second time. This time, he actually read it and his mind was completely blown away.

Billy exclaimed, "When I bought my very first property in New Jersey, my wife and I were in Cairo, Egypt. I remember signing from my hotel room and how amazing it was. I just picked up this property and subsequently took control over my financial life while 5,967 miles away. From there, I started getting better results. Next, I started speaking with my friends who were here in Spain. I started talking to friends who were in the United States, and I was just completely geeking out on everything I was learning."

In 2016, after Billy started having personal success with his long-distance investing, his friends became interested and wanted to be able to invest with him. Initially, he pushed back and said he couldn't help, but as he thought more about it, he realized he was in a great position to help others achieve their financial dreams. He reached out to a couple of lawyers in Europe and back in the United States and put it all together and created his company, KeePon Cashflow. His mission is to build a strong bridge between investors in Spain and surrounding countries to profitable cashflowing properties in the United States.

"It was one of the biggest and probably the scariest moment of my life. At the same time, I really felt I was able to now serve someone, and we've been able to continue to do that over and over again. We've been able to continue to serve other people. In December 2020, we actually had our very first investor that has entrusted us with their confidence, to the point of one million dollars. It is one of the things I am absolutely humbled by because you are having someone entrust their dreams and goals with you. It's one of the things I feel so humbled and fortunate to be able to continue to serve other people."

IMPLEMENTATION

As you can see, you can leverage many different strategies as a single-family real estate investor to be successful. Are you more of an active or passive real estate investor? Buying turnkey will take a lot longer to build wealth than the BRRRR method since you won't start with 20 to 25 percent equity from day one. However, if you make a high income and don't have the extra time to find off-market deals, the turnkey strategy may be the best for you like it was for Doug. Maybe you are interested in becoming a private lender like Shannon. Therefore, it is imperative for you to understand your strengths, your limitations, and your ultimate goals for your future. These honest answers will drive you to the best strategies for you based on your overall wealth goals to ensure you're successful.

I encourage you to set your passive income goals and consider the dollar amount you would like to generate monthly and by what time frame. Is it having $5,000 per month of passive income by the age of fifty or sixty? Maybe it's having $20,000 a month in passive income by next year. Regardless, set your SMART goal and begin taking daily actions to achieve it. Next, I recommend you consider starting a journal to write down all your goals daily and ensure your actions follow. Next, determine how many single-family homes you need to meet your passive income goal? From there, you will need to determine how much cash flow to expect from a single-family home in your target market. Once you complete these steps, you must commit to analyzing deals on a weekly basis and making offers to get the next deal under contract. Next, we will discuss the benefits of fix-and-flips and wholesaling.

CHAPTER 10

FIX-AND-FLIP & WHOLESALING

———

*"Real estate offers huge financial advantages
to those who will learn the system."*

GARRETT SUTTON

If you're reading this book, I am almost 100 percent certain you have seen at least one fix-and-flip TV show. Whether you watched Dave Seymour's *Flipping Boston* show or Christina and Tarek out in LA on HGTV's *Flip or Flop*, you are familiar with the concept of "flipping" a house. You find a discounted piece of real estate; you buy it, renovate, and sell for top dollar in a few months. I admit they make it look easy and straightforward mixed in with a little extra drama. I have been flipping homes since 2015, and I promise you my truck has never been stolen, my house has never been spray-painted, nor have I been surprised that I needed a new roof on the place! According to *Forbes*, the profit margin of a successful fix-and-flip ranges anywhere between $40,000 and $70,000 for the average residential home. In our market, we aim to profit at the very least $30,000 for a single-family renovation project. Fix-and-flipping homes isn't trivial, but with the right mentorship and systems it can be made simple and very lucrative.

The other strategy we will cover in this chapter is wholesaling, which is nothing more than becoming the middleman in real estate transactions. As a wholesaler, you market to motivated home sellers, negotiate a deal and get it under contract, and assign your rights to purchase the house to an investor for a nominal assignment fee. Assignment fees can range from $500 to five or six figures, depending on the size of the deal!

These are both great strategies to build businesses or as even just a small side hustle. I started house-flipping as a side hustle since I have a great job in the Air Force that I love, but I wanted to build additional capital to buy more rental properties for passive income. If you are busy, flipping one or two houses is better than none. It's also a great way to get started in real estate. Adam Grant, in his book *Originals*, states entrepreneurs who keep their day jobs have 33 percent lower odds of failure than those who quit their primary job. The decision for me wasn't too risky as I manage complex projects for a living. However, it still took a leap of faith to put my money where my heart was. Flipping real estate requires one to learn the fundamentals of evaluating home values, estimating construction cost, project management, and overall team building.

Our company has grown over the years to where we are on track to execute fifteen projects in 2021, managing a virtual team fourteen hours away in sunny Panama City, Florida. It will be a learning experience to orchestrate all the different disciplines involved, to go from getting a deal under contract to selling to a buyer after renovations. I leverage the same evaluation principles laid out in the previous chapter on single-family investing when it comes to flipping. In my *Millionaire Real Estate Success Strategies* course, I break the entire process down into three simple steps: Find, Fix, Finish. These basic principles are part of every real estate deal to include my next story, highlighting one of our fastest selling and most profitable flips ever!

$70,000 PROFIT IN FEWER THAN SIXTY DAYS

You always hear people exclaim money isn't essential, or it isn't the most important thing. I agree. If you have enough money and aren't in a distressed situation, it's not most important. If you think about it a little deeper, whenever there is an abundance of anything, we tend to not pay it much attention. Conversely, whenever we operate from a place of necessity or need, our focus and awareness are heightened to do whatever possible to solve the pain point.

This principle remains valid in buying and selling real estate, too. I saw this firsthand with our purchase of the Palmetto house. Panama City was still recovering from the devastation caused by Hurricane Michael, and the real estate market was in shock from the lack of inventory. At that point in time, we were full steam ahead in our marketing campaign to get more deals under contract and do our small part to help the community rebound. Our most recent contract, the probate house, resulted from our new bandit signs and taking action to place them in strategic locations all over the city. Before we could even close, the seller felt comfortable enough to give us a referral to a friend looking to relocate soon. Referrals are a great way to find deals. This allows you to avoid starting cold with building rapport with a seller. She gave me the couple's phone number, and I set the appointment.

I showed up at the appointment and I was pulling up to the house, and I was like, "Wow!" It had a couple of pieces of loose siding upfront, but it was primarily a brick home with vinyl siding features along the front and the side of the house. As I approached the front door, I said to myself, *This is a $400,000 house with higher holding cost, or the cost incurred while owning a property until it's sold.* We previously had a renovation project at that same price point in the Mountain Brook area of Birmingham, Alabama. It took nine months to sell due to a combination of contractor challenges, season change, and being at the top of the market. When you're dealing with a property nearly twice the price of the average home sold in the market, there aren't as many buyers who can afford to purchase the home.

Immediately after walking into the spacious living room, I could tell there wasn't much work to be done. We continued to walk through the house, and she explained a little more about their situation and the need to relocate to Salt Lake City, Utah. They needed to be there by early May since her husband had a firm date to start his new job. Unfortunately for them, they had to sell this house before closing on their house in Salt Lake City.

There it was! Their primary motivating factor was to sell their home at a discount. Sometimes, sellers aren't as straightforward and motivated, and you must dig and pry to determine the underlying motivation. This was the most important thing to them, but I didn't pick up on it then. Her husband didn't say much during the walk-through, and I could tell she was taking charge and the primary decision-maker.

I told her point-blank, "You guys can sell this house on the MLS with a realtor and make more than what we can pay." She told me she knew we were in the business to make money and asked us to still give her an offer. We went outside to the backyard, and there was a little work to do on the outside, and we continued to the porch, and then there was a beautiful pool in the backyard! I wrapped up the appointment, provided some additional information about my company, discussed other homeowners we helped, and let her know I would be in touch soon.

After I got back to our beach rental, I told Melissa how everything went, and by that time, after doing a quick assessment, I decided, based on my own limiting belief, that this house was a no-go because they wouldn't accept an offer around 70 percent of the after-repair value. The next step in the deal flow is the follow-up after you have dug into your numbers. So, I went and did my analysis, and everything was coming back with an after-repair value of $400,000 to $425,000. Based on that price range, we were down in the low $300,000 range with our offer price. I just knew there was no way they would sell for that amount. At that point, I wrote it off and moved on to something else before even having a follow-up conversation with the seller.

During that time, we were living out on 30A—a great stretch of beautiful, sandy beaches tucked inside a quaint little upscale beach community. We were still living there as we waited for our house repairs to be completed. It was toward the end of February 2019, and I could remember sitting in the living room chair hanging out with the kids, looking out the window when my phone rang. It was her calling me back after waiting for three days. I answered the phone. "Hey, Johnny, I was just following up to see if you had a chance to do what you need to do and see where your offer was for our house," she said in an excited voice. So, I swallowed and hesitantly responded, "I think we're gonna end up probably somewhere around $310,000, but I haven't got the comparable sales back from my realtor." In a straightforward, matter-of-fact kind of voice, she said, "Okay, I think we might be able to work with that number and get it done."

I hung up the phone, and I was floored! I thought, *The Lord works in mysterious ways*, and started working to double-check my numbers to make sure I wasn't overlooking anything. I double-checked the average days to sell in the Panama City, Florida, market for all homes $350,000 to $450,000, the prices per square foot, ensured all the homes were similar age, lot size, pools versus no pools, and my assessment for our estimated repairs. From my research, I knew they owed close to $283,000 on the house. Based on all my analysis, I conservatively settled at an offer price of $305,000. A couple of days after work, I met with her in person and told her that after performing my due diligence, we ended up with an offer of $305,000 for the house, and she agreed.

We ended up closing May 2019 right on time, leveraging a hard money loan. They closed on their new house two days later just as they hoped! It was a true win-win situation.

The project went as planned! Fix...We only put $5,000 into a couple of minor repairs to the house. Yes, only $5,000! It was nothing super creative or game-changing that led to the extremely low renovation cost. It signifies how frustrated the homeowner was with managing repairs and ready to be rid of the headache. We repaired the exterior siding along with the front, second-story window and side gables of the two-story house, the back porch screen, touched up the ceiling where there was the water stain, and that was it. I went and bought a floor shine product, and we mopped the hardwood floors ourselves, and that was it!

We listed the house for $400,000 in only two weeks after making only $5,000 worth of repairs and received an offer from a Facebook ad. The buyer's realtor came back with a full-price offer. After receiving the property inspection report, we negotiated and ended up settling at $15,000 off the list price, and we sold it for $385,000 in a little bit less than sixty days. Money isn't always the number one factor for everyone. I had heard it and read it before, but this confirmed it. Initially, I had limiting beliefs on what someone would sell for and almost talked myself out of one of our most profitable deals to date. They could have easily sold their house for $350,000 to $360,000 by just listing it on the market with any realtor, but they were looking for a set time and the proper timing to get them on with their life in Utah. It taught me to go into every discussion with a homeowner looking to better understand what their challenges are and how we can best serve them and craft a win-win solution for both of us.

Another interesting part of this deal was that we didn't use a realtor to sell this house. All along, I was planning to use a flat-fee MLS service to list the house on the MLS, and we operate as the realtor. We had previously purchased nearly a dozen houses at that point in our lives and were comfortable with the process of not having a realtor represent us. Only two weeks after purchase, I went over on a Friday to put our Operation Restore "For Sale" sign in the yard. It was a proud moment. It would go live on Monday with the flat-fee service, but I wanted to place an ad on Facebook since I had recently performed some trial-motivated seller ads. For this one, I just ran a weekend teaser ad titled "Coming Soon" with the Palmetto house pictures.

That Sunday morning, we were getting ready to go to church, and I received a text from a realtor saying he wanted to see the house, so I gave him our lockbox code. A few hours later, he came back and said he had a local pharmacist looking to buy a house and that this house was perfect for his family. We sold this home in less than sixty days from the day we bought it and walked away with a $70,000 profit! Never forget, money isn't always the most important factor to every motivated seller.

TERMITES AND THREE BUYERS LATER

Next, I want us to dig a little deeper into the fix-and-flip project we covered back in chapter 8 from Justin Melendez. We walked through how he partnered with family members to purchase this project in Fayetteville, North Carolina, that involved a wholesale deal, termite damage, and three separate purchase contracts.

Justin picked up the deal from a local wholesaler and the sellers were three relatives who inherited the property that was going into foreclosure. On top of that, one of the family members had a criminal offense and owed money to the courts, which caused the wholesaler to give up his assignment fee to keep the deal alive.

From the beginning, Justin told me he likes to have a home inspection up front before closing. I used to use this same strategy when I purchased properties virtually. Also, he has his general contractor (GC) walk the property. "We knew what we were getting into throughout the inspection; we found just normal stuff that you see in older houses. There was evidence of termites in the garage. After we received the termite inspection from the termite and pest control folks, they let us know there's quite a bit of termite damage under the house." Justin shared the inspection document with his GC, so he could see the areas with damage. He didn't account for the additional damage, which added an extra $2,000 initially.

He didn't do any additional due diligence throughout the whole six weeks leading to closing. "I've seen people not go back out to the property and become pleasantly surprised when they close on the house and there's a tenant in there suddenly, or the AC unit is missing, and then they're just in a world of hurt. So, I'd recommend that day of closing if you can't, then have somebody else look. We had a $25,000 rehab budget that we planned for, but my GC came back, with the termite damage, with a total estimate of $21,000. So that was great. He finished the project; we fixed all the termite damage in the garage. He addressed termite damage in the crawlspace. However, he repaired the crawlspace in only one spot, and not throughout the crawlspace. So, I never went in the crawlspace because I don't like crawling in the crawlspaces at all."

Justin had given him the diagrams and the inspection reports and expected him to just read through it and fix everything there, but he didn't! "We were live for like three days. This was at the beginning of the COVID inventory shortage. We received four offers within the first three days. We received a $180,000 offer with a $10,000 appraisal gap guarantee. At the same time, I'm leaving for work for training, and my training requires me to not have my phone, so I was glad we got it under contract."

Justin's realtor was also his GC. The next week they are notified that the buyer performed their inspection, found a ton of termite damage, and decided to back out. His realtor relisted the house back on the market. A day later, another awesome offer comes in; not $180,000, but $142,000. This buyer performed an inspection, and they backed out because they saw the same termite damage! The GC/realtor decided not to fix the damage before relisting the house while Justin was out of the local area at training. They were closing in on four and a half months for the project with an additional thirty to forty days every time they go under contract. His realtor claimed the first buyer didn't provide the inspection report and just said they were backing out because of their inspection report but with no details. The second buyer told him what was wrong with the termite damage. Unfortunately, it took him about a month and a half to get the termite damage fixed due to his realtor's busy schedule.

Once again, they secured a new buyer quickly. They went through the entire process with the buyer and had a good inspection with only minor due diligence repairs requested to the amount of $1,000. Unfortunately, during the last week, they backed out because the buyer failed a drug test and lost his job. He could no longer close on the deal. "When they backed out, it hurt, man! This one tested our resolve. We were closing in on five and a half months. I decided to go through it one more time. I talked to my investors to let them know what was going on. They never once questioned the contractor or me. But they knew that I had it under control. So that was good. And an important piece I should say with investor relations is that at every turn, at every contract failure, at every due diligence report, they were informed as much as they wanted to be."

They received another offer the fourth time, a conventional offer at $157,000 with 20 percent down. They finally closed the deal just over the six-month mark, and at $157,000, they initially underwrote it at $131,000. Overall, the deal ended up having a return on investment (ROI) of 40 percent for him and his brother! "It was a hell of a project. It took a long time, and there was a lot of back and forth. I thought it was just going to go smoothly when I left for training, but it didn't. I call it the REI monster, the real estate investing monster; he's always out to get you. But that's what you get paid for. The issues, we have to manage them." This is so true. Some projects are easier than others, but you must hold fast and see the project through for yourself and your investors when adversity strikes.

MY FIRST WHOLESALE

Now, let's talk about wholesaling for a bit. Wholesaling is nothing more than becoming the middleman connecting a seller and buyer. Wholesaling isn't real estate investing since you never own the property, but it remains a great way to build capital to invest in real estate. The barrier to entry is extremely low, which allows anyone to get started. Regardless of where you live, owners are always looking to sell a property "as is" without using a realtor. Additionally, investors are always in every market looking to buy discounted real estate to add to their portfolio or to flip.

To be successful, you must be able to find buyers and understand their buying criteria, so you can seek out the right type of deals that meet their requirements while simultaneously seeking out motivated sellers with properties that meet the buyer requirements. Once you find the right property, you essentially go through the same steps of fix-and-flipping to evaluate the property. After evaluation, you negotiate a fair purchase price that allows you enough room to add your assignment fee while allowing the buyer enough equity to still make a decent profit. Once you have saved enough capital from assignment fees, you can start keeping deals to either BRRRR to add to your rental portfolio or flip to bring in a larger amount of capital.

The lifeblood to wholesaling is marketing to motivated sellers. Your marketing can be as simple as getting a free, tax-delinquent list from your local tax assessor and writing handwritten letters or personally visiting local owners to discuss the property. Alternatively, it can be as elaborate as hiring an ad agency to run advanced campaigns leveraging multiple media such as Facebook and Google. It primarily depends on your budget and the target audience you are trying to reach. Within real estate, multiple niches allow you to focus on a specific audience, or in this case, a motivated seller. As I mentioned earlier in the book, I started buying a couple of rentals and then transitioned into fix-and-flips to generate more income. However, upon moving to Panama City, Florida, in the summer of 2017, I began to do wholesale deals too.

We moved to Panama City, Florida, while finishing up a virtual flip in Birmingham, Alabama. We purchased another foreclosure as a primary residence, and our Birmingham remodeling team came down for a few weeks to do the work since we hadn't established a local team yet. By the time we completed the renovation and had gotten settled in, there were rumblings of a deployment tasking that I was one of a few who were qualified to fill. I hadn't deployed since 2011, so I was overdue for another deployment. We experienced a lot of success virtually flipping in the Birmingham market, and we were ready to finally be in a local market where we could be more hands on, so getting tasked to deploy was a tough blow to our business plans. However, we had already begun marketing locally, so we kept marketing and began to gain traction with local sellers. My training started after Thanksgiving, and there wasn't time to build a team. So we decided to wholesale.

We placed a considerable down payment on our foreclosure purchase since we couldn't use our VA loan again due to a lack of remaining entitlement. We deployed a large amount of cash reserves on the renovation cost. So, wholesaling allowed us a quick way to replenish our cash reserves. Our first wholesale came from a bandit sign. Bandit signs were a great source of leads in our market, but they were considered a code violation in certain local townships. Make sure you understand your local laws before you start hanging bandit signs all over town! The seller was a local landlord who had just foreclosed on a property he had owner-financed years earlier. He didn't want to renovate the property again and was ready to sell. It was in bad shape, but it had potential.

I didn't have a network of local cash buyers, but I had recently gone to a local real estate meetup where I met a few investors and realtors with whom I could share my deal. I started to call other wholesalers/investors with their bandit signs up around the city looking for deals. Doing so, I hit the jackpot! I found a local couple who were looking for deals, and they had a motivated buyer list. We decided to partner, and I agreed to pay them $3,000 for bringing me a buyer. I was able to assign the deal for $11,000 in less than three weeks. It was a win-win deal for the seller, buyer, my wholesale partner, and me. Being resilient and understanding how to analyze deals helped me successfully broker the deal. In the remaining three months leading up to my deployment and in between training, we successfully wholesaled five deals from a fire-damaged trailer to a 1940s brick cottage.

IMPLEMENTATION

Fix-and-flipping and BRRRRing a home is by far the most hands on when it comes to real estate investing. When flipping a house, one of the largest downsides remains the amount of money you have to pay in taxes unless you have a solid tax strategy in place. With a good mix of selling and buying rentals within the same year, you will be able to offset a nice size of your tax bill. However, I am not an accountant, so please seek the advice of your CPA for what's best for your situation.

Every house and project is its own canvas and brings its own unique challenges when it comes to renovations. I am of the data-driven investor camp and lean on what the data is telling me when it comes to list price, interior finishes, materials, and time required to sell. Sometimes you will hit a homerun with a job with a light rehab and large profit spread, and others you will run into termites, delays, and personnel issues along the way. Do you have the time to venture into completing your own fix-and-flip project or to become a wholesaler? As an investor, your job is to manage your risk as much as possible through your upfront analysis and due diligence. You make money in real estate when you buy, not when you sell. The life of an entrepreneur and real estate investor is a roller coaster.

This is one of the reasons why I love mentoring and teaching other real estate investors how to run a successful real estate investing business. For most of my investing career, I didn't have any mentorship or anyone to lean on to ask questions. However, I was able to lean on my technical, project management, and leadership skills to achieve success. Ultimately, my goal is to help shorten the learning curve and the mistakes made by new investors to ensure success.

I teach them the systems/strategies I put in place in my business and mentor them along the way as they execute and implement. We cover it all: marketing, negotiations, finding team members, renovations, raising capital, sales, and a host of other topics! Have you thought about who you already know that would be great on your team? If you charter a flight to fly to Aruba, would you jump in the pilot seat with no training, no copilot, or no map? Of course not! So, why would you go into building a business without any mentorship or guidance from an expert who's been there and done that? In our next chapter, I will discuss the strategies centered around apartment—aka multifamily—investing.

CHAPTER 11

APARTMENT INVESTING

———

"If everyone is moving forward together,
then success takes care of itself."

HENRY FORD

I can remember back in my college days at The University of Alabama and the first time I moved off campus into an apartment. The complex was huge and strictly allocated for college students, with most of the units having four bedrooms and two bathrooms and a common living area and kitchen. The units were rented by the room for $600 per room which equated to $2,400 in rent per door in a complex that had sixteen three-story, twelve-unit buildings! This equated to a staggering $460,800 of income per month.

At the time, I couldn't even imagine how many millions of dollars it would take to own a property of that size, and I never would have envisioned being able to own it! We all have limiting beliefs on what we can accomplish in life. It took many years to overcome those limiting beliefs when it came to money and investing. My prayer and goal for you is this chapter shows you the different ways you too can add apartment investing into your portfolio whether as an active or passive investor.

It took me stepping out of my comfort zone and attending a multifamily investor conference to realize how attainable owning an apartment truly was. It also showed me the level of teamwork involved to be a successful multifamily investor. Apartment investing has more sophisticated underwriting techniques and more expenses due to the number of units and management considerations when executing a business plan. However, you can hire, partner, or outsource those areas where you aren't strongest to properly manage the apartment. Essentially, buying an apartment is nothing more than buying and operating a business. Let's look at a great multifamily investor, Mr. Rey Reyes, who transitioned from retiring as a lieutenant colonel after serving twenty-eight years in the Army to become a full-time multifamily real estate investor.

RETIRED ARMY OFFICER TO FULL-TIME MULTIFAMILY INVESTOR

I had the pleasure of sitting down with Rey when visiting Orlando while putting my book together. I met Rey a year earlier at a multifamily conference, and we routinely ran into each other at virtual meetups. As a second lieutenant, like so many real estate investors, Rey was impacted by reading Robert Kiyosaki's *Rich Dad Poor Dad*, and it changed his entire mindset about money and investing. Early on he bought a few single-family homes but realized he was impacted by the inability to make progress when he wasn't physically present. Rey was another long-distance investor and even bought single-family rentals from overseas, but he realized the one flaw with single-family rental properties. If you're looking to generate a large amount of passive income, you would need to buy a lot of good deals, and finding good deals can take a lot of time!

In the military, depending on your specific job or career field, you may be stationed overseas for multiple years at a time or even deployed in a war zone for nine to twelve months straight. Your single-family rentals require you to have a property manager to manage your portfolio. You will need to lean on them to show the property to potential residents, hire contractors to make repairs when things break and most importantly, collect rent. Additionally, your revenue or income is derived from a single-family asset that generates zero income when vacant.

Knowing this, Rey pivoted to investing passively in both multifamily investments using his Self-Directed IRA and through private lending to hard money lenders. "When you compare the multifamily aspect to single family, nothing beats the scale of multifamily on the residential side. For me, it's more of a time aspect. It takes a certain amount of time to go through an acquisition. A multifamily acquisition takes maybe twice as long as a single-family does, but you're going from one unit to four units, or from anywhere from fifty to one hundred units plus. So, it was just a matter of trying to figure out how fast I wanted to get somewhere and single-family investing was just going to be too slow."

Rey is right! Syndication provides more economy of scale and opportunities to grow your wealth without being hands-on for it to be successful. Partnering with knowledgeable apartment operators lowers your risk and allows you to invest in larger deals that you wouldn't be able to typically afford if you tried to invest in them alone. You can participate as a limited partner or private investor with no operational responsibility. However, as with all good syndicators, we keep our investors informed and send out monthly or quarterly newsletters with updates on our business plan execution. We ensure our investors stay up to date on the overall performance of the projects and the performance of our property management team, so they aren't left guessing on how their asset is performing.

As I mentioned, Rey is a full-time multifamily syndicator and operator focusing on value-add multifamily properties across the Southeast US. Currently, his company has acquired 401 total units with a valuation of over twenty-eight million dollars. I asked Rey if he could go back to when he was eighteen years old. What would be his advice for himself? "I would say at the very least, you need some level of preparation for yourself, and certainly, you need to have some money. If I started saving just a little bit earlier on, it would have been useful and would have helped with the progression.

"Do something to prepare yourself! In multifamily syndication, you can be part of a team that has something to offer, and you don't want to be the one person trying to jump into a team, but you don't have the skill set to at least be in that space. You don't have to be the smartest or the best but bring some individual focus and consider putting more money away as you go, since I didn't do it, and I know a lot of other people don't either."

APARTMENT INVESTING METRICS

So, I know you are probably wondering, what makes a good apartment deal? Well, it depends! It depends on your strategy and investing goals. Some apartment syndications plan for as short as a two-year hold period, some may go as far out as seven to ten years, or you may want to buy an apartment and keep it forever! Every apartment deal is different, but most offerings advertise anywhere from 6 to 10 percent cash-on-cash return a year with a target internal rate of return (IRR) from 15 to 20 percent. As a benchmark, a 20 percent IRR essentially doubles your principal investment in five years.

Most syndicators focus on value-add apartment deals where the current owner has deferred maintenance at the property and hasn't kept rents at the market rate. Coincidentally, it becomes hard to charge premium rents if the property hasn't been renovated over time. There lies the opportunity to buy an apartment at a discount to execute a business plan to renovate units over a set period and increase the rents as the units are transitioned. It seems simple enough, but every apartment isn't the same.

One of the primary variables that drive asset price or capitalization (cap) rate for a market is the location. Cap rate is used in the world of commercial real estate to indicate the rate of return that is expected to be generated on a real estate investment property. Cap rate is based on the net income the property is expected to generate and is calculated by dividing net operating income by the property asset value. The location determination is driven by future projections for job and population growth in the local economy and surrounding areas along with crime statistics, school ratings, access to major transportation arteries, etc. One of the current trends that will be with us for at least the next few years is the mass baby boomer migration. We are seeing thousands of baby boomers relocate to the Southeast United States for retirement. Additionally, many people are escaping high-income tax states such as California, Illinois, and New York for states such as Phoenix, Florida, and North Carolina.

THE DEAL I NEVER KNEW WE COULD DO

I referenced our first apartment deal a few times in the earlier chapters to amplify several different concepts. Real estate investing is a continuous journey where success evolves as you grow in knowledge and experience. I didn't venture into multifamily until 2020 after over a decade after buying my first single-family home. I knew apartments had many benefits and economies of scale, but I was so focused on single-family properties that I never took the time to see how close I was to make the transition. It didn't hit me until I attended a multifamily investing seminar in Orlando, Florida, back in October 2019.

I try to attend at least two professional real estate investing events or seminars every year. Unfortunately, in May 2019, I tore my ACL in my left knee, which had to be surgically repaired. All my summer plans were altered, forcing me to miss my scheduled events. So, after a summer full of physical therapy and rehab, I was excited to find a real estate event coming up in Orlando, Florida, where my sister lives. So, we made a family trip out of it; I went to my seminar in the day while the family hung out and enjoyed each other.

The event was life changing! There were hundreds of apartment syndicators, operators, and private investors from all over the US with all levels of expertise represented. Additionally, a couple dozen well-known syndicators and operators gave presentations across the two-day event. A few of them I had the pleasure of interviewing for this book. Some guys had portfolios of apartments in the thousands of units! Some had quit full-time jobs making six figures, and others were operating part time so they could eventually leave their day jobs. One of the immediate trends that stood out to me was the emphasis on team building to be successful.

I left that conference with new inspiration and a vision for my investing journey. My new goal was to purchase our first multifamily property within the next year. Who would have known I would underwrite and submit my letter of intent (LOI) to purchase our first multifamily in less than forty-five days in December 2019! I found the deal while searching on the MLS for the sales price of a vacant commercial lot behind our duplex as we prepared for its refinance appraisal. The apartment was owned by two older couples, with both owning other businesses while eyeing retirement. The apartment was listed for $1,350,000 and on the market for over ninety days at that point. I underwrote the deal and submitted an LOI for $1,000,000, which was my first seven-figure offer ever. I would walk the property a month later, and it would not be until early March before we would get it under contract. We closed in June 2020 in the middle of the COVID-19 pandemic.

My wife and I decided to manage the property ourselves for five months since we already had orders to relocate back to the northern Virginia area before Christmas. My mindset was to gain valuable experience managing the property to assist with gaining more insight into operations to better manage the property management companies on our future apartment deals. It was a great learning experience as I worked directly with our residents as we all navigated COVID-19 and maintained some type of normalcy.

I have heard horror stories from other investors about how their residents banned against them and stopped paying rent due to the eviction moratorium. We were blessed not to have to experience those issues. However, we did have a couple of residents lose their job during the pandemic and struggle to keep current on payments, but from day one, we let our residents know we would work with them however we could, so we all could get through the pandemic together. At the end of the day, our residents are part of our team, and one could argue the most important part. Our mission is to provide clean, quality, and affordable housing for our residents. From day one, we demonstrated this by catching up on deferred maintenance and making necessary repairs to improve our residents' quality of life.

One of the unique parts of our apartment purchase was the fact of us taking over an active insurance claim for four of the units damaged by Hurricane Michael back in October 2018. This allowed us to not have to worry about having an additional $50,000 for renovation. Unfortunately, it took eleven months before we would settle with the insurance agency on the cost of the renovations. It was a hot mess that led to some of the sellers' motivation. The short story is the owners signed an assignment of benefits and trusted a contractor who mismanaged the renovation project. The site lead quit on the job, taking all the historical documents leaving his company owner in a bad spot. During this timeframe, the onsite contractor demolished and removed a lot of cabinetry and flooring before the insurance company had an opportunity to come out to take pictures and officially assess the damage. Subsequently, the insurance company had to hire third-party engineers to assess the damage and generate reports for the field adjusters in order to complete their final report.

Fortunately, it all worked out in our favor to have the claim paid out. Once we renovate the four units and return the property to 100 percent occupancy, we will perform a cash out refinance into a long-term low, fixed rate loan. We spoke back in chapter 8 about inflation. In our business plan before purchase, we estimated rents at $850 a month. With inflation and a shortage of rentals, in June 2021, our market resided at $900 a month. Our estimated monthly income will be around $15,000 per month with monthly cashflow after expenses and debt service (mortgage payment) of about $5,000.

THE WORLD CITIZEN INVESTOR

Next, I want to share the story of a phenomenal individual and mentor I look up to, Mr. Maurice Philogene! I met Maurice through networking and attending different meetup events. He is an authentic human being focused on being the greatest version of himself while assisting others in achieving their dreams. His family is originally from Haiti, and he was born in New York and raised in Boston. After attending the University of Virginia, majoring in engineering while playing football and participating in Air Force ROTC, he ended up in the DC area working for a consulting firm where he still works today. He recently retired from the US Air Force after a twenty-two-year career. Fortunately, the year he graduated, too many officers graduated nationwide, so he went into the Guard Reserve since his consulting firm offered him $42,000 a year, and the Air Force would only start him as a second lieutenant at $24,000 a year.

He ended up as a federal agent working in the Air Force Office of Special Investigations, essentially working two careers. In 2002, he jumped into real estate after buying a place to live, which was the beginning of the boom cycle in the 2000s. Over the next six years, he would buy thirty-five single-family homes he self-managed. "The beautiful thing that ended up happening was I learned over time that if I paid off these single-family homes, I would create passive income. And that passive income would be greater than the salary at my firm, and I wanted freedom! The reason I did it was because I wanted to control my time; it was never a money thing. It was always about controlling my time, so I could go do those things that you and I just talked about, which was traveling around the world to experience life the way I wanted. That's kind of how the business track started."

After continued success in single-family investing, Maurice made the transition to multifamily in 2015. "It wasn't because I was trying to become this massive company; it was because I stopped growing as a person. I was pressing repeat for fourteen years, and I'm grateful that I did it; we're pressing repeat for fourteen years on buying single-family residences, mostly condos and taking revenue from the military, revenue from my consulting firm, revenue from rents and paying off the first one, and then doing it again, paying off the second one, and this snowball effect happened to the point where I had eighteen paid off places, so I was fine financially. But I wasn't challenged by any of that."

So, Maurice went into a real estate investment program and got a mentor. It took him about two years to break through his internal limiting beliefs that he could be successful in multifamily investing. He did his first deal, which ended up being a syndication. Fast forward to today, thirty-plus deals later, he is helping other people get to the five freedoms his business coach taught him, financial freedom, time freedom, geographic freedom, freedom of purpose, and freedom of relationships. "So, I wanted those five freedoms. What I'm doing now, by working with investors who are trying to get into real estate, it's not that they are necessarily trying to become millionaires and billionaires; it's that they're trying to have the lifestyle that they think millionaires and billionaires have!"

It's just a bit of time freedom and the ability to unplug from the nine-to-five rat race, not get caught up in titles and ranks, and compete with your peers. His company, Quattro Capital, established in 2019 with three other partners, has grown exponentially. They have purchased over eighteen apartment complexes across nine different states totaling over $100 million in 2021 alone. He also sponsors aspiring investors and thus far, through his mentorship, he assisted new investors in closing seven complexes and parks over the past two years. Lastly, Maurice has been blessed to travel to over ninety-six countries throughout his life journey and provide lasting impacts across the globe.

FROM TV STAR TO PRIVATE EQUITY FUND MANAGER

I'll end this chapter on apartments by finishing the story about Dave Seymour after landing his star role on A&E's *Flipping Boston*. "The TV show opened up a lot of doors for me. The doors that most guys and girls would knock on, and they won't get an answer. For me, the TV show was the key, and if you put that key in the right door, it can open a lot more opportunities. It was national exposure on the *Today Show*, Rachael Ray, Squawk Box, and CNBC since people wanted to hear my opinion, which always cracked me up. You're asking me about these big deep, business-oriented questions, and two years ago, I was helping save heroin addicts who had overdosed. For me, I was always present and appreciative of the gifts that have been given to me, so I never squandered them with stupidity, and I sought to follow good people."

Dave built a portfolio of cash-flowing real estate the entire time he was flipping houses on the TV show. Once he dialed it in and figured out the cashflow game, that's when things really began to accelerate for him. He also spent a lot of time in the lending business for real estate through hard money lending coupled with some private lending. "It was a great business model and continues to be if I like a deal personally. When I liquidated everything and looked at the landscape that has been created with COVID, the lending business was out of business in approximately three days because Wall Street stopped buying at no origination." It was a crazy time!

From there, Dave transitioned and reconnected with Walter Novicki, who has been investing in real estate since 1986. "He is a fantastic individual, an unbelievable friend and partner. When it hits the fan, in any scenario, you want Walter by your side. He and I met in the education space we were teaching together with a national company, and we were the older guys on the road in our early fifties. We were hanging out with the kids who were being stupid at night. It was good, but we found there were a lot of commonalities and trust between us, so we launched Freedom Venture Investments, a private equity fund company."

As of mid-2021, they were in the process of wrapping up a one-hundred-million-dollar raise to buy multifamily assets in the Gulf Coast region of Florida, which is what his partner Walter has been doing for over twenty-five years. When COVID-19 came along and kicked everybody in the teeth, as Dave so eloquently stated, they saw the coming opportunity to assist amateur apartment investors facing challenges due to eviction moratoriums and not having the necessary reserves to run the properties effectively. Most didn't have proper property management and are experiencing higher than normal vacancies coupled with low rents.

They only deal with accredited investors, individuals whose income is $200,000 a year or more as an individual or $300,000 as a family unit or a million dollars in net worth, as determined by the SEC. Becoming an accredited investor is a simple process with your accountant or attorney signing off on your accreditation.

Dave discussed obtaining a letter recently for an upcoming investment he was making. "I just got an accredited letter for myself for an investment I'm making with one of the

New England Patriot players who have a new headphone business. I like his business, and I get an opportunity to hang around NFL players. So, for $50,000, I'll take a seat at the table and make a couple of bucks on these headphones, but being accredited gets you some exposure to investments that most other folks don't receive. However, the minimum investment in our fund is $100,000, with most of our investor conversations center around $250,000 to $500,000.

"It's a good business, and I'm very proud that Walter and I have never lost one dime of investor capital in over twenty-five years of our careers. It's because we're probably the most conservative mothers on the face of the earth because we're now working with other people's retirement dreams and other people's children's college savings. We take it very seriously. I want to relate to my investors, and I don't take a dime into my fund until they talk to me first. I want to meet my investors and know what their goals are to make sure we're aligned. I'll decline if they don't align with our family values. Our ideal investor is somebody who wants to come and play in the real estate sandbox, have fun, and get a fantastic return along the way."

Dave is 100 percent right about the faith and trust investors place with the apartment syndicator's ability to deliver the promised returns. It's a serious business but a rewarding business as you meet more investors and hear their stories and dreams. As we move into the future, with the aging of baby boomers and the increasing trend of millennials choosing to rent more, apartment investors will continue to beat the stock market and secure great cashflow and appreciation in the future.

IMPLEMENTATION

Investing in apartments is a whole new world for those who aren't ingrained in it daily, but at the same time, it's no more than multiple small single-family homes co-located. As with any business, you will only be as good as your employees or team members. Have you considered or are you interested in investing in apartments passively or actively as a syndicator? If not, you should because it's one of the best cash-flowing, tax-advantaged assets, period. However, it is important to choose the right general partner or investor team to align with before investing.

There are many eight- and nine-figure super syndication teams, but some great, smaller syndication teams only focus on certain markets and have a lower investment minimum. At the end of the day, you want to align yourself with a team that has the same values as yourself. Therefore, I align myself with other syndicators like Jerome, Maurice, John, Rey, and Dave, who make their investors priority number one! We recognize the sacred responsibility that comes with managing millions of dollars on behalf of our investors. I encourage you to seek out more information on multifamily investing to see if it's a good vehicle to diversify your portfolio and help you accelerate achieving your retirement goals.

CONCLUSION

YOUR ROADMAP TO SUCCESS

"Success doesn't bring happiness. Happiness brings success."

SHAWN ACHOR

We have come a long way since chapter 1, read some great real estate investing stories, and picked up habits of successful investors. We also covered the real estate strategies necessary to build long-term wealth and achieve *your* American Dream. America is abundant in wealth, and it is now your time to go forth and achieve the wealth that has been set aside for you. The gap between the haves and the have-nots in this country continues to widen each day. So, it's not a shocker that nearly half of all Americans have no retirement savings, yet there is a lack of financial literacy taught in our schools. It goes without saying; I'm not optimistic it will be changing any time soon.

This was one of the primary reasons I decided to write this book. I wanted to share and give back some of the knowledge that I and other successful people I know have found and use daily to achieve success. I always look back to just how much I didn't know about investing after I earned a piece of paper qualifying me to be able to work a job for someone else's company. It took me ten years, but I remained disciplined and committed to achieving success in my life in all areas, from my relationship with my family to buying and selling millions of dollars in real estate every year.

We spoke a lot about the skills needed to become successful in life, but for me, it always pointed back to my faith in God and my belief in His promises for my life. Promises of peace, joy, love, and prosperity because the Bible says you have not because you ask not. As Steve Harvey says, "If you up your ask, then He will up his give."

I love giving back to the next generation because so many people poured life into me becoming successful in life. It pains me to see the path to success and freedom for so many others, yet the motivation and sense of urgency are not reciprocated. We are constantly bombarded with negative news and distractions on social media that can rob us of our precious time if we aren't careful.

Overall, there is a shortage of mentors, which are critical to the success of our next generation. My mentor and friend, retired Colonel Alvin Burse, told me success is a simple recipe. It's something anyone can do since you don't have to be the smartest person in the world, nor have all the money in the world; you don't need any of that stuff. All you need is ambition.

I wholeheartedly believe anyone can become successful in life and real estate if they simply put their mind to it. As

Tony Robbins said, success is 80 percent psychological and 20 percent skill or talent. Once you decide to make your goals of achieving financial success and securing generational wealth for your family a must and not a wish, you will be successful. Rod Khleif spoke with me about success, and he said, "Motivation gets you started. Commitment will bring you home. And it can't be one foot in one foot out either. You're either all in or you're all out. That's the way it works."

We talked about the facts behind how most millionaires have made their millions through real estate and how many millionaires today are self-made. I originally had the belief that more millionaires inherited their wealth. This fact helped me think through formulating a strategy to help my children become properly positioned to take my efforts and successes to the next level after I'm gone and to secure wealth for my grand and great-grandkids. Success no longer means working for a single employer for thirty years, climbing up through the ranks, and retiring. Success is less about earning a decent wage and more about being entrepreneurial in nature with a hybrid approach of commingling both work and personal lives.

We dove into the number-one key to real estate success is to take action. We only have a finite amount of time on this planet, and we can't procrastinate and waste any more time. You must manage your focus because focus is power, and where your focus goes, your energy flows. If you can achieve incredible focus, you have incredible success in whatever you focus on. A great quote I grabbed from my sit down with Rod Khleif was, "Successful people focus on their strengths and hire people to cover their weaknesses." He's 100 percent correct. Don't waste time focusing on weaknesses when you can hire experts to perform those tasks since you will probably never achieve their level of proficiency. My good friend Anthony Moore shared with me one of his mentor's thoughts on acting. He said, "If you're not failing, or if you haven't failed at your job, that means you're not trying hard enough and you're not innovating."

We took a look at having grit to persevere and overcome obstacles and challenges that we all encounter at some point in life. We discussed the importance of networking with other like-minded people and the power of masterminds. Jim Rohn said, "We are the average of the five people we spend the most time with." Real estate is the ultimate team sport due to all the different functions to make a deal successful. In the Air Force and the military in general, we focus on building dynamic and high-performing teams to accomplish our mission of air superiority. As a successful real estate investor, you must determine your strategy, operational goals, and tactical tasks to build the proper team for real estate investing superiority.

The last third of the book was dedicated to mission execution and demonstrating key real estate strategies you can leverage to become successful. We walked through numerous stories of how others have achieved success in each real estate niche we covered. For any new real estate investors, I recommend you focus on one niche to master to prevent distractions and ineffectiveness. We started by discussing a myriad of ways to finance real estate deals—from obtaining traditional bank financing to financing deals through a self-directed retirement account. We went through the benefits of investing in single-family rental and how to evaluate deals. Also, we covered the nuances in successfully flipping a property and how to wholesale a deal. Lastly, we covered how to invest in apartments and syndicate an apartment deal. Apartments allow a great economy of scale, and they allow investors to create large amounts of passive cashflow faster than buying individual single-family homes.

Personally, it has been a challenging yet rewarding experience bringing all the personal stories and stories from other investors together to hopefully inspire you to achieve greatness. It was a constant balancing act to dedicate time away from the family to write and interview people while working full time in my Air Force job and running our real estate business. Additionally, about a month before my draft manuscript was due for initial review, my mom took ill and passed away. I contemplated stopping and taking a complete break for a moment, but she always taught me to finish whatever I start, and a man is only good as his word. In the end, if this helps one person achieve success, it was all worth it.

At this point, no excuse is left for not achieving your success in real estate. You have the roadmap and hopefully the internal fuel to get you there. It won't always be easy, but it will be well worth it. If you're looking for more details on how to get started and implement these strategies in your personal situation, feel free to join my real estate investing community to surround yourself with like-minded investors working to achieve success through real estate investing. If you are interested in partnering with us on any of our future apartment or single-family deals, you can sign up and join our investor club. You will be part of our VIP group who receive notification as soon as our deals go live to secure one of the limited positions. For both opportunities and our additional information and free resources, simply visit www.JohnnyLynum.com. I wish you much success in all your future endeavors, and remember success isn't something you pursue. It's something you become!

ACKNOWLEDGMENTS

___

If you read this book all the way through to the end and have landed on this page, you should be acknowledged. It's been quite a journey writing this book. It almost didn't begin after I laid out every reason why I was too busy to both my wife and Professor Koester. I had to take my own advice and become comfortable being uncomfortable. It was tough juggling the interviews, weekly lecture time, finding the time to write, all while being a present husband, father, son, brother, working full time, and leading a family business. I couldn't have made it through without my family's love and support. This was especially the case after losing my mom, Ruth Lynum. She was my rock, motivation, and biggest cheerleader.

Johnnie Lynum Sr., aka J1, thanks for molding me into the man I am today. You and Mama set the bar high for my life, and you gave me daily, living examples. All those Saturday mornings dragging me away from cartoons to come with you to work were well worth it!

Melissa, thank you for always pushing me to greatness and believing in me!

Johnnetta, thank you for always riding with me and supporting everything I touch!

J3, Mackenzie, Jace, and Chloe, thank you for being the best kids a father could ask for! This book is your roadmap to life and the key to unlocking all your dreams. Be sweet and go get it!

Uncle Melvin and Uncle Leon, thank you for those monthly seeds of money you blessed me with as I pushed my way through college. It means a lot to me!

Nick Battle, thanks for pushing me to buy my first house! No one could have imagined it would lead to all this.

Thanks to Lemus Santiago and the team for all their hard work and expertise! You are the wheels to our bus!

To the team at New Degree Press, thank you for providing a platform to bring my book to life. Professor Eric Koester, thank you for not taking no for an answer and providing enormous value in every one of your lectures. My developmental editor, Collen Young, and my marketing & revisions editor, Kathy Wood, deserve special thanks. Thanks for your feedback, your sharp eye, your steady commitment to keeping me accountable to myself, and your constant reassurance.

Thank you to all my interviewees; your stories and experiences provided invaluable insight into what success looks like. Each of your stories are a testament of your courage, resilience, and greatness:

Alex Breshears	Larry Powell
Anthony Moore	Maurice Philogene
Billy Keels	Mandy McAllister
Brian Briscoe	Rey Reyes
Courtney Ervin	Rod Khleif
Dave Seymour	Roderick Robinson
Doug Spence	Shannon Kiefhaber
Jerome Myers	Spencer Hilligoss
John Casmon	Vinney Chipora
Justin Melendez	Yonah Weiss

And a massive thank you to everyone who pre-ordered *Millionaire Real Estate Success Strategies* and made its publishing possible: Eric Koester, Davonya Bouatene, Ashley Bynes, Lance Hayes, Eddie Lewis, Tommie Chapman, Alietha Howze, Dosia Mcbride Jr, Icee Strain, Latanya Hudgins, Rory Compton, Eric Johnson, Stephane G. Bouatene, Justin Melendez, Wistaria Joseph, Mark Linder, Brian Rogers, Larry Powell, Shelia D. Lynum, Justin A Mitchell, Taja Nix, Jermaine Sailsman, Nichole King-Campbell, Arthur Earl Dent III, Tres Ledson, Stephen O. Ejide, Claude Labbe, Andrea Jeffers, Kevin Taylor, Dalian Washington, Clayton Hollinhead, Doug Spence, Jeffrey Wright, Lawrence Barron II, Remon Bradley, Kiffany Ray, David Wilson II, Tremaine Wilson, Cedric Lynum, Roderick Robinson, Johnnetta Clemons, Ivy Strain, Stephanie Wilkes, Dr. Janet D. McMiller, Lauren Lynum, Tawona Davis Marshall, Shonta M. Ezell, Jamie L. Welch, Marques Jackson, and Joseph Learthur Flagg Jr.

APPENDIX

INTRODUCTION

Fearless Motivation. "The Inspiring Story of an Old Watch and Self-Worth." August 26, 2021. https://www.fearlessmotivation.com/2020/07/16/the-inspiring-story-of-an-old-watch-and-self-worth/.

Horowitz, Juliana M., Igielnik, Ruth, & Kochhar, Rakesh. "Most Americans Say There Is Too Much Economic Inequality in the US, but Fewer Than Half Call It a Top Priority." January 9, 2020. https://www.pewresearch.org/social-trends/2020/01/09/trends-in-income-and-wealth-inequality/.

Sightings, Tom. "7 Myths About Millionaires." November 29,2018. https://money.usnews.com/money/blogs/on-retirement/articles/7-myths-about-millionaires.

United States Government. "Gross Domestic Product, 1st Quarter 2021." May 27, 2021. https://www.bea.gov/news/2021/gross-domestic-product-1st-quarter-2021-second-estimate-corporate-profits-1st-quarterChapter.

Wiggins, James. "Millionaire Investors Name Real Estate as Most Popular Alternative Asset Class by Wide Margin." February 6,2014. https://www.morganstanley.com/press-releases/millionaire-investors-name-real-estate-as-most-popular-alternative-asset-class-by-wide-margin_404f321a-29ad-438c-afab-ff18ceb302ac.

CHAPTER 1

Boateng, Grace. "Mikaila's Magic: How an 11-Year-Old Girl from Texas Became an $11 Million Dollar Entrepreneur." Accessed September 5, 2021. https://forwardtimes.com/mikailas-magic-11-year-old-girl-texas-became-11-million-dollar-entrepreneur/.

Glink, Ilyce & Tamkin, Samuel. "A Breakdown of What Living Paycheck to Paycheck Looks Like." Accessed May 23, 2021. https://www.washingtonpost.com/business/2020/08/17/breakdown-what-living-paycheck-to-paycheck-looks-like/.

Jeffrey, James. "The 13-Year-Old Who Built a Best-Selling Lemonade Brand." Accessed September 5, 2021. https://www.bbc.com/news/business-44860428.

Lusardi, A., Oggero, N., & Yakoboski, P. "2017, The TIAA Institute-GFLEC Personal Finance Index: A New Measure of Financial Literacy."

Report on the Economic Well-Being of US Households in 2017, available online at www.federalreserve.gov/publications/default.htm.

Zapp, Daniel. "Money Matters on Campus." Accessed August 28, 2021. https://everfi.com/wp-content/uploads/2019/05/MoneyMatters-2019.pdf.

CHAPTER 2

Napoleon, Hill "Chapter 2." In *Think and Grow Rich—Napoleon Hill*. Primento Publishing, 2011.

Robbins, Tony. "The Psychology of a Winner." Accessed May 30, 2021. https://www.tonyrobbins.com/stories/coaching/the-psychology-of-a-winner/.

Thomas, Eric. *"The Secret to Success: When You Want to Succeed as Bad as You Want to Breathe."* Atlanta: Spirit Reign Pub., 2011.

Veterans United Home Loans. "VA Loans." Accessed October 10, 2021. https://www.veteransunited.com/va-loans/.

Yates, Johnathon. "90% of World's Millionaires Do This to Create Wealth." February 11, 2020. https://thecollegeinvestor.com/11300/90-percent-worlds-millionaires-do-this/.

CHAPTER 3

Blank, Michael. Essay. In *Financial Freedom with Real Estate Investing*. Archangel Ink, 2018.

Kagan, Julia. "Collateral." Accessed October 11, 2021. https://www.investopedia.com/terms/c/collateral.asp.

Kyle, Kath. "10 Goal Setting Statistics: Research Studies Facts & Findings." Accessed on June 8, 2021. https://www.kathkyle.com/goal-setting-statistics/.

Lieberman, Charlotte. "Why You Procrastinate (It Has Nothing to Do with Self-Control)." Accessed on September 5, 2021. https://www.nytimes.com/2019/03/25/smarter-living/why-you-procrastinate-it-has-nothing-to-do-with-self-control.html.

O'Donovan, Kristin. "4 Reasons Taking Action Is Crucial in Achieving Success." Accessed on June 7, 2021. https://addicted2success.com/success-advice/4-reasons-taking-action-is-crucial-in-achieving-success/.

CHAPTER 4

Hayes, Steven. "How to Take Action When You Don't Wanna." Accessed October 3, 2021. https://www.psychologytoday.com/us/blog/get-out-your-mind/201802/how-take-action-when-you-don-t-wanna.

Jakes, TD. "TD Jakes on Finding Your Purpose." Accessed May 13, 2021. https://www.tdjakes.com/posts/t-d-jakes-on-finding-your-purpose.

Robbins, Tony. "What Motivates You to Take Action?" Accessed May 13, 2021. https://www.tonyrobbins.com/productivity-performance/what-motivates-you-to-take-action.

Young, Scott. "How to Push Past Your Analysis Paralysis." Accessed April 21, 2021. https://www.scotthyoung.com/blog/2019/01/28/analysis-paralysis/.

CHAPTER 5

"Accountability" *Merriam-Webster.com*. 2021. Accessed September 4, 2021. https://www.merriam-webster.com.

Doran, G. T. (1981). "There's a S.M.A.R.T. Way to Write Management's Goals and Objectives." Management Review, 70, 35–36.

Gardner, S., Albee, D. (2015). "Study Focuses on Strategies for Achieving Goals, Resolutions." https://www.dominican.edu/sites/default/files/2020-02/gailmatthews-harvard-goals-researchsummary.pdf

Jordan, Michael, and Vancil, Mark. *I Can't Accept Not Trying Michael Jordan on the Pursuit of Excellence*. San Francisco, CA: HarperCollins, 1994.

Kleingeld, A., van Mierlo, H., & Arends, L. (2011). "The Effect of Goal Setting on Group Performance: A Meta-analysis." *Journal of Applied Psychology, 96*(6), 1289-1304.

Patterson, Melanie. "The Best Hard Money Lenders for 2021." Accessed on September 5, 2021. https://fitsmallbusiness.com/best-hard-money-lenders/.

Siegle, Del. Help Students Set Goals. Accessed on October 5, 2021. https://nrcgt.uconn.edu/underachievement_study/self-efficacy/se_section8/#.

CHAPTER 6

Duckworth, Angela. *Grit: The Power of Passion and Perseverance*. New York, NY: Scribner, 2018.

Larson, Brita. "Grit: What It Is and How You Can Learn It." Accessed October 8, 2021. https://centerhealthyminds.org/join-the-movement/getting-into-the-nitty-gritty-of-grit-what-it-is-and-how-you-can-learn-it.

Myers, Jerome. "Fraud, Flood, Fire and a Pandemic." Podcast audio. Accessed August 3, 2021. https://podcasts.apple.com/us/podcast/fraud-flood-fire-and-a-pandemic-randy-langenderfer/id1505610992?i=1000530830574.

CHAPTER 7

Kaufman, Wendy, "A Successful Job Search: It's All About Networking." Accessed September 9, 2021. https://www.npr.org/2011/02/08/133474431/a-successful-job-search-its-all-about-networking.

Peck, Sarah. "Why Your Most Important Business Move Might Be Joining a Mastermind." Accessed June 10, 2021. https://www.forbes.com/sites/sarahkathleenpeck/2018/02/21/why-you-should-join-a-mastermind/.

Robbins, Tony. "What Is a Mastermind Group." Accessed September 9, 2021. https://www.tonyrobbins.com/business/mastermind-group/.

CHAPTER 8

Biggerpockets. "Robert Kiyosaki: Rich Dad Poor Dad. Author Predicts a Crash." Podcast audio, September 2, 2021. https://youtu.be/4qU8n1xNp3k.

Campisi, Natalie. "How Buying a House Can Hedge Against Inflation." Accessed June 23, 2021. https://www.forbes.com/advisor/mortgages/homebuying-can-hedge-against-inflation/.

Misko, James. In *How to Finance Any Real Estate*, 145–145. Garden City Park, NY: Square One Publishers, 2004.

CHAPTER 9

Chen, James. "Turnkey Property." Accessed September 15, 2021. https://www.investopedia.com/terms/t/turnkey-property.asp.

Nowacki, Lauren. "Understanding The BRRRR Method of Real Estate Investment." Accessed September 15, 2021. https://www.rocketmortgage.com/learn/brrrr.

Nyitray, Brent. "American Homes 4 Rent Is My Favorite Single-Family Rental REIT." Accessed September 15, 2021. https://www.fool.com/investing/2021/05/25/american-homes-4-rent-is-my-favorite-single-family/.

Pierce, Justin. "Why Single-Family Houses Make Better Investments than Apartment Buildings." Accessed June 5, 2021. https://www.washingtonpost.com/business/2020/08/24/why-single-family-houses-make-better-investments-than-apartment-buildings/.

CHAPTER 10

Grant, Adam, Sandberg,Sheryl. *Originals How Non-Conformists Move the World.* New York: Penguin Publishing Group, 2017.

Saurabh, Shah. "The Advantages and Disadvantages of Fixing and Flipping Real Estate." Accessed September 16, 2021. https://www.forbes.com/sites/forbesrealestatecouncil/2021/06/21/the-advantages-and-disadvantages-of-fixing-and-flipping-real-estate/?sh=2be1c4152d94.

CHAPTER 11

Chen, James, "Capitalization Rate." Accessed June 24, 2021. https://www.investopedia.com/terms/c/capitalizationrate.asp.

Frey, William. "How migration of millennials and seniors has shifted since the Great Recession." Accessed June 24,2021. https://www.brookings.edu/research/how-migration-of-millennials-and-seniors-has-shifted-since-the-great-recession/.

Moussa, Feras, "Four Reasons and Three Ways to Begin Investing in Apartments." Accessed June 22, 2021. https://www.forbes.com/sites/forbesrealestatecouncil/2021/04/12/four-reasons-and-three-ways-to-begin-investing-in-apartments/?sh=22ac467a648a.